REDEMPTION SONGS

A Trilogy of Poetry

Julian Thomas

AuthorHouse™
1663 Liberty Drive, Suite 200
Bloomington, IN 47403
www.authorhouse.com
Phone: 1-800-839-8640

First published by AuthorHouse 3/11/2009

ISBN: 978-1-4389-4958-1 (sc)

Printed in the United States of America
Bloomington, Indiana

This book is printed on acid-free paper.

authorHOUSE®

Oh Pirates, yes they rob i
sold i to the merchant ship
minutes after they took i
from the bottomless pit.
But my hand was made strong
by the hand of The Almighty.
we flowered in this generation
triumphantly.
Won't you help to sing
these songs of freedom?
Cause all i ever had
redemption songs.

--Bob Marley

MY WORLD

BOOK ONE:

THE EARLY YEARS

This book is dedicated to my mother,
who always taught me to follow my dreams.

There are no revelations from God to the unready
—Socrates

Thank God for our illusions, they're all we've got
—Twain

Remember always:

learn from Paul the art of allusion
learn from Saul the art of metaphor
learn from Amiri the art of thought pattern
toss in the spicy eternally classic feel of Gwendolyn
with the rhythm and beat of Langston
and you got some funky poetry

but acquire the raw wisdom of James
and you will be timeless
the spiritual beauty of Kahlil,
the maturity of Maya. . .

-- Joules

INTRODUCTION:

Word

What is there beyond the poetry
beneath the lines
in between the pages

Before metaphor and simile
before even the letters themselves
there was and is
the word

ask not what the word can do for you but what you can do for the word

but what can I do for the word

word

word

word man

do you know the word man

say word man

and ecoutez bien

this is for the young heads, the ones that run with the dread poets
who dropped their lowest lotus blossom positions on wax
and packed the streets that brought back break beats
their spirits peak 93 million miles away from the streets
away from the leeches that sucked dry young dreams
while entertaining visions of power like a crack fiend
the hungry tired and poor
holy sacred and pure
ready to plant seeds in bushes of thorn
ready to fuse the word with the form

for all of the revs ready to take it to the streets
not reverends, but revolutionaries packin heat

armed to the teeth
willin to die for their meat

for all of the people tired of feasting on sand
and ready to take their hood back to the motherland

for the millions tired of payin bills with government paper
tired of watchin the red white and blue rape your artwork
steak their claim in your heart's birth
its seven fold worst

aborting possible missions with mid classed sterilized incision
slicing your veins with military precision

whoever's made the decision to turn a new leaf

increase the peace and spark trees to condone it

a new world alliance
and this is for those ready to get up on it

from the teenage mother strivin to get out of the tenth grade
sellin her body with one more heat bill to pay

to the young vicelord desperately climbin out of the south side
with dreams much bigger than just gettin high

for the b-ball players who don't want to be role models

and the old classmates still nursing the same 40 bottle

for those still hoping to plow their mule and 40 acres

the 12 year old c-note makers

the premature life takers

to the graduates dissatisfied with their sheet of paper

this is for the black owned corner store riot looters
the six in pipe shooters
and the classmates who never shared a coke or a smile
with those six students in lower Colorado

for every boy forced into manhood without a father

for all of the people who ever needed a reason to leave their mark on the world

and for all of those who ever doubted me

this book is for you

let you light shine 'round
the world, my brotha
your light shine around
the worl-ld my sista
let your li-ight shi-ine a-round
the world ev'ry body
let your light
shine
round
the
world

word

Defining Moments

The poet goes 'round makin ends meet by beatin suckas over the head with sound, bangin tuning forks on minds, lookin for vibrations that don't stop with time.—Paul Beatty

Reality ain't always the truth.—KRS-One

The Spot

a place to be
a place for me to stop and think of what i see
this is what i need
a place with peaceful serenity
distilled patience
and steady beats
where the deafening silence awakens the mind
where the chaotic stillness stops all time
here i can can create whatever i choose
here is where the unheard tune comes alive
a place for me to be me
unhindered
a place to be

How To Relax

close your eyes and think
think of a quiet comfortable place
where you can be

away from the noise
away form the crowds
away from the restless rhythms of life's stormy chaotic sea
it may be a tiny cozy little place
or a field stretching to wide open space
go there once and you'll never want to come back

breathe in
and slowly let it out

with closed eyelids see the past day's
events steadily tr i c k l e   a   w   a   y
with closed eyelids see yourself
finally lacking motion
truly begin to float away
you can see a lot with closed eyelids
but only if you know what you're looking for

breathe in
and slowly let it out

feel a tingling sensation begin
at the very tips of your fingers
let it ripple all throughout your body
sip a cool drink if you have one
and embrace the icy liquid
with first your lips
then your tongue
then your throat
as you help it cool you to the core

breathe in
and slowly let it out

think of pleasant things
of family and friend s or your one true love
think of all the joy they bring
or perhaps think of nothing at all

let a cool soft breeze tickle your nose and cheeks
smile at the thought of how good this all feels
and then enjoy it some more

breathe in
and slowly let it out

listen
and for the first time truly hear the sounds of the world
the silent stillness grows and grows until at last it shatters
the blackness of what you thought you were seeing
in spills reds of the brightest vesuvian fires
blues of the most clear caribbean seas
lush fields of panamanian green
browns of the richest earth of mother Africa
and every other hue and tone imaginable
all floating in a slow motion view of what you called life

it seems so simple
from this point of view
and you wonder why you never saw this before

breathe in
and slowly let it out

My World

midnight in t-town
and i'm clinging onto
a serene slumber

i
the dreamer
travel to an ideal land

troubled by a nation that only grows weaker
i conjure up a foreign world
and take notes for future plans

the natural poet that i am
causes my pen to never cease
and like a thelonius monk
in a mysterioso land
i travel in peace

spotted a place where everyone
practiced what they preached
and each sermon had a quote
from the bible of brotherhood
kind version of course

and even though nobody there knew my name
i still felt like cheering all the same
as i watched a land emerge
where the only status quo was acceptance

and the small percentage sharing my minor hue
although relatively few
were no longer seen as a threat of civil disobedience

finally a home where the buffalo soliders could freely rome
the mud stained plains of the wild wild test of time
that history lessons place on young children's minds

minds left tainted by false pictures of the past
strategically omitting certain lessons from class

lessons of roots
that connect the vines of yesteryear
with the fruit of tomorrow

and like an ali-fraiser rumble in the cerebellum
these wide-eyed pupils are bobbin and weavin
and not even believin endless harangue
of professor david duke

so they ignore the pain

and eagerly await the anti self hate study groups
crammin' to pass this week's love lesson:
care for your neighbor as yourself
guaranteed blessin

and teachers find themselves possessin'
the time to teach what's really important
since here they are the highest paid profession

the world no longer blind to the fact
sees that no sum of money could pay a teacher back
for educating our future
bridging our past
and stabilizing all the in between

nevertheless they do accept an increase in the green

and then i ran into a man overjoyed at the sight
of no longer embodying a national plight
no blazing fire
or racial muck and mire
followed his trail to every job interview

like langston he too sang america
but the darker brothers who made it thru
were no longer plagued by the chanting drums
beaten by new workplace chums

"oh, he's so articulate
he's not like the others
he just speaks so well"

meanwhile youth who dwell
 on the underprivileged side of the tracks
no longer face the strife of a hard knock life

trapped in the high stakes game shows
of cultural jeopardy
win loose or proselytize
and wheel of immorality

where the only way to win these games is to not play

and that was never an option

and then i noticed that *eracism*
was more than a t-shirt
here it was a way of life
for the offspring of baby boomin' idealists
whose impact on the world made a difference after all
sparked a drive for peace in all
and started a coalition truly rainbow
in thought as well as living color

hand in hand they marched
thru poverty and thru greed
thru jealousy and thru ignorance
and all the fires of dissention
that place man against man

and from the dying embers
rose the sweet vibrant smoke of serenity
stretching out to all corners of the land
creating a universal love more supreme
than coltrane could ever dream

and then

and

then

i woke up

smiling

at what might

one day be

reality

The Beat

always has been
always will be
always is
the beat

in many shapes forms and sizes come the steady rhythms
whose pulses keep the beat of life

out from the back waters of our heritage
our essence
our very being
come the pulsating gyrations that keep life inevitable

meanwhile, the beat goes on

on a small corner a little girl crouches beneath a front stoop and cries
daddy's leaving home now
and all she can do is sit and watch
can't listen anymore

she used to listen to the rhythms
her parents would make in their bedroom at night
syncopated rhythms
not rhythms of love
but rhythms of wrath
and all she can do is sit and watch
as daddy is handcuffed and driven away

meanwhile, the beat goes on

somewhere in a dark alley
a group of young hustlers waste the night away
sipping their e&j as they swear over dice games

their mothers can only nod their heads in despair
their pastors can only try so much
their wives can only cry so much
their brothers can only die so much

meanwhile, the beat goes on

Jam Session

the set laid out
battered instruments in hand
our music was
like a fiery mexican jalepeno
like a '69 camero finally unleashed
like the vegas strip on friday night
it was the japanese bullet
and beethoven's fifth
all rolled into one
and then we were done
and its like leftover turkey a week after christmas
like someone at the last of the hot fires
and left the empty bag in the cupboard
like a mahjong hustler in oklahoma
without any tiles

Message to A Black Man:
An Open Letter to Louis Farrakahn

you son of a ...
traditional episcopalian
an underground derailing
of good ole fashioned
christian values
deep seated resentment
time not well spent
usin' and abusin'
your hatred of a percent
ranging in this changing land
around 2.2
yet you yourself are lineage
from a portugese jew
who knew
a detroit ghetto dwellin youth
would one day be
such a mighty conquerer
with speech and voice
smooth as a bassline from mingus
a kahn in your title but far from genghis
a mind hiding inner loathing
or is it fear
the message you send is far from clear
but it sounds so good
movin' and a groovin'
round a forked tongue
that shades so much
clouding over words
that might do harm
perhaps the charm
that you posses
comes from the stress free
experience in door to door salesmanship
if only the coats you so contentedly sold
could protect from your reign of hatred
dietary health freak
prime for the weekly fastings your nation calls for
neo-black-islamic
but isn't it ironic
that your great predecessor

turned his back to face the east
before the fated insurrection
rose thru the ranks
under x's direction
yet spine shattering conspiracy
is all we see
not the love
you so warmly preach
espousing esoteric speeches
with incendiary messages
your day of atonement
left us begging for more
so we whooped and hollered
and went home with dollar-dollar
plans of c.r.e.a.m.
convinced that we too
were a part of the american dream
yet your dreams never deferred
even at the beginning of the word
the word was with you
and the word was made you
as you gripped for the torch of the nation
sleek as it may be
but the word is Allah
and not wallace d.
the chosen one is who you claimed to be
maybe ...
but the vast majority in this land
can't begin to understand
the line between love and hate
and that you've drawn between you
and your fellow man
us and those like you
see the plentiful work you do
cleaning up slums
scratching hell of backs
and extendin' a hand to all those who in need
there's plenty of silver lining in this cloud
and we believe
an original man
casting aside names from slave days
yet would elijah turn in his grave
if he knew what his bright young
slim-faced, fair skinned
enchente grinned
fiery, yet eloquent pupil
was up to today

louis we love you
but don't lead us astray

Untitled

everybody's got one
but where is the proof
unneeded
we just believe
wars are fought
executions occur
the persecution of many
the ideas of a few
we all do our jobs
we just believe

Midnight Rhythms

see it
smell it
sense it
as only you can
reach out and touch infinite warmth
a lover's embrace beneath a silver moon
time to slow down the hands of time

breathe it
inhale
exhale the sweet kiss of life
the spices of love
the funk of passion
the quality of life

enjoy it
become it
live it

let me show you the cosmos
and all the gifts that come along with it
spinning pulsars and churning galaxies
caught in the universe that we call love

the universe that's only known to you and me

the only one that matters

reveal the secrets of your galaxies
and i'll show you endless heights of ecstasy
ones that you could only call heaven

open up the mysteries of your solar systems
show me the power of your atmospheres
let me hear the brightness of each new dawn
as your sun rises over your budding planets

unlock the key to the depths of your deepest sea

show me your darkest secrets

i'll clear away any scarred moon
or any chipped comet that may be left over from the past
remember, comets always disappear in the end
and moons are in constant revolution

the quality of life

enjoy it

become it

live it

be it with me
and together we will reach
new plateaus of sensual evolution

share my universe
and we will transcend this reality
of war and hate
and jealousy and wrong

this land of self pity and material love

this planet that only supplies an uneven equality

and justice that's conditional at best

transcend reality

echappez-la avec moi

(escape it with me)

Autumn Leaves

leaves of the fall
rest now
your day is surely done
let peace and calmness rim your brow
your time of ease has come
i'll wrap you up in my black bag
with millions just like you
your once soft tips have lost their sag
from drops of morning dew
leaves of the fall
be still for me
for it is a cold november
past spring days will remain free
as long as i promise to remember

Tomorrow
(for my graduating class)

is me
is my time to shine
is my time to be me
and to cross my very own lines
drawn out of fear
of failure

i must be led and taught
i must be inspired and brought to the table
so that i can pick and choose what's best
instead i've been labeled as generation x

generation x

x as in unknown

   we don't know what these youngin's are gonna do
   so we better just leave them alone

and so they do
and so we go
out into the world to learn what we need
to survive and grow

so don't be surprised at what worldly things we know

don't be surprised at what we reap
cause its already been sown
by other neglected disrespected people just like us

and if we can't reach out to you
what do you expect from us

we all need to be touched

that's what makes us the way we are today
that's what makes us do the things we love to do
and say the things we love to say

our cries for financial help from parental units
leave us handicapped
caps in our hands demanding
whats not rightfully ours in the first place

a mind
hell, a job is a terrible thing to waste

so waste not want not
as the saying goes

        but i'm too cool to be lectured at
        too smart to be told

        so if you don't like me
        cause you don't care for my style of hair

        if the way i dress makes you nod your head and stare

        if listenin' to my music makes you feel sick

        or you can't see me cause your mind can't switch

        from the old days
        former ways
        past time type of shit

        then we're gonna have problems

who am i

i am unheard voice of a thousand high schools
my cry goes out from every corner of the nation

verbalized thru acts of gang warfare and civil unrest
emailed to america thru stories of overdoses on crack and heroin

faxed to the world thru abundant s.t.d.'s and babies havin' babies
the message is clear and there is a present danger

who am i

i am the lost soul hoping
groping for a home that isn't there yet
by the time it finally gets there my mind is already set
by the time i started high school i knew what kind of adult i'd be
and if you haven't done it by now you'll never reach me

you'll never teach me to push my talents
to the edge of my skills
to expand my mind until it will never fill
to shoot with my intellectual license to kill

who am i

i am the bridge to the future
connecting the world with what it could should and would be
if it weren't for the churning waters below
threatening to drown me

destined to sweep hotel lobbies
just because i never learned that i am somebody

who am i

i am youth
in every broken hearted story

calling out to anyone with ears to listen
to help this fellow man

well tomorrow never dies
but today sure can

today sure can get caught up in the hype of young livin'
wastin' away our time
and the precious minds
we been given

looking
seeking
waiting

for someone else
perhaps a stronger person than yourself
to get you out of this cycle
work for you
and produce your wealth

come on man
funk dat!
get a life

the mountain of success can only be climbed
through hard work and strife

strive for excellence
shoot for the moon

and when you make it
don't forget where you come from
and make yourself look like a bufoon
have your melon steadily swellin'
like a circus balloon

for that person looks around
and he soon learns
a forgotten past makes waste of all you have earned

whatever happened to the days of peaceful rap
of the daddy mack
with backward slacks
when a friendly dance wasn't a cardinal sin
can it be
was it really
all so simple then

too many hopes unheard
too many dreams deferred
too many unsung heroes forgotten and cast aside

too many troubled minds fighting battles
from another time

too many broken spirits
forcibly movin' on down that line

people are left feeling hopeless and helpless
so the rule stays true
watch your back

and if you can
keep that one track mind
on the right track

so whachu sayin' black
red, yellow, brown, white too
tomorrow is a day we must all look forward to

its not just for you
and its not just for me
tomorrow is a day
 for every race and every creed

a day when you seek me
when you seek me
when you find me

and i becomes we

we grow
we learn
we loose sometimes
but we earn our right to live
our place in the sun

you better get with it
cause the race is not won by the swift
nor by the strong
but by the one who moves to the beat of his own song

our drum beats passionately
like a raging fire within
but don't let it consume you with ignorance
ignore that whim
that desire for what does not
will not
and can not last
take a step beyond the cozy confines of your own class

sophomores
juniors
seniors

we're all freshmen to the world

so who are we

who are we

we are youth

and this is our story

but it hasn't been written yet

so all you writers of dreams that vibrate and move
all you directors of wishes that tend to soothe
al you actors shooting for broadways debuts
don't waste time brooding over critics' reviews

you gotta be you
gottabeyou
got
ta
be
you

cause if your'e not you
then who are you
and what can you do

tomorrow is a day when we yearn to be free
to glide on the winds of hope gracefully
soaring on outstretched icarus wings
we fail to see that our time for unpunished recklessenss
is nearly done
blinded by our own pride
and lack of faith in older ones
missing in wisdom
our rebel definace
melts into shadows
upon the sun

things fall apart
the center can not hold for long

its time to write a brand new song
to create a home where we belong

it's a battle to the death
but we're already winning

and this is not the end
but only the beginning

finally
finally the gateways of time
tomorrow is here

it's our time to shine

Upturned Bridges

what do i care how the world sees me,
i'm only trying to figure out how i should
feel about myself. —Mingus

The world's a dream,
not because that dream is a falsehood
but because its truer than it seems.—Basho

Wild Side Lounge

if you're here for an english 101 lesson
on the literary profession
or a starbucks cafe luncheon
with scholarly discussion

then you're in the wrong place

if you're here for a 3 keg drinkin'
brain cell count sinkin'
one half night standin'
underhanded romancin'
rum and coke spicin'
freaknik enticin'
night on the town

then you're in definitely in the wrong place

this here's the wildside lounge
where hungry poets scrounge and scrap for
artistic meals to feed their overwhelming hunger

and seek out open mic sessions
that let us teach lyric lessons

rhyme and reason force artwork into university treason
droppin' verbal shells that keep our clientele bleedin'
and its always huntin' season

students be actin' fowl
so we maintain our midnight prowl
in search of a campus home
that we can truly call our own

written words come to life when spoken aloud

calling all poets
calling all poets

calling out to all you writers
dreamers

believers
teachers and preachers
professors of wisdom
protectors of expressions
guardians of creativity
craftsmen of vision

all you muses
lyracists
catchers of dreams
verbal musicians
composers of passion
keepers of the faith

calling out to all you poets worldwide

hope you're ready to get wild
as we put our verbal smack down

cause for one night only
the circus is in town

hey y'all
look around

the circus in town

the circus is the town

and you never get out of town

The Revolution Will Not Be Computerized

you will not be able to stay home brother

you will not be able to plug in, switch on, and cop out

you will not be able to open chat rooms
and idly have cyber sex with people who think you're thirty because
the revolution will not be computerized

the revolution will not be computerized

the revolution will not come to you
in four charming colors for your imac 2000

the revolution will not be designed by bill gates
or a highly trained team of software engineers
who graduated from m.i.t. magna cum laude
just so they could make enough ends meet
to afford the latest upgrade of final fantsasy 18
or the entire james bond 007 collection on dvd

the revolution will not be computerized

the revolution will not come to you
in the shape of a lab top console

it will not have an address that begins with a w w w dot
or a website that will not bill your card
but needs the number simply for age verification

the revolution will not have a seven letter keyword
they revolution will not send you forwarded chain letters
the revolution will not have instant messenger because
the revolution will not be computerized, brother

there will be no excite files of hidden federal financial aid
uncovered by agent molder and agent sculley
as part of the y 2 k cover up

or a how to beat the l-sat program available on cd rom

your daily horoscope will not be able
to predict your grade point average
when venus enters full retrograde
and the winter solstice begins

the revolution will not be computerized

there will be no last minute cram sessions at the 24 hour starbucks
there will be no last minute cram sessions at the 24 hour starbucks

there will be no e mails of late term papers to sociology professors
with notes attached describing the funeral in chicago
you simply had to go to

the revolution will not be computerized

there will be no downloaded versions
of your american lit novels
read out loud by james earl jones
and newly available on mp3

mouse pads
bookmarks
and u s b ports
will no longer be so damn relevant

and freshman will not care to waste time
forwarding all their friends the latest in cartoon porn
because students will be in the parks
looking for better ways to spend their afternoons

the revolution will not be computerized

the revolution will not be delivered to your door
with 12 monthly payments
or have a two year warranty with a fifty dollar rebate

the revolution will not be made payable
by check or money order

the logo will not be designed by microsoft
or pentium plus

there will be no software compatible with windows 98
netscape navigator, webzone, lycos, or yahoo

the revolution will not be computerized

the revolution will be no super highway accessible to you
at the double click of a .com .org or a .edu

you will not have to worry about an ethernet hookup
the surge protector in your wall
or the kilobytes in your modem

the revolution will not have digital enhancement

the revolution will not have a flaming logo with a personalized home page

the revolution will get america back on line

the revolution will not be computerized

will not be computerized
will not be computerized
will not be computerized

the revolution will be no saved hard drive, brother

the revolution will be live

A Few Haiku

steel silver bullet
rocks gently and steady through
howling bitter wind

soft vein filled petals
stretching for the rising sun
cast off night's grey dew

through thick layered clouds
sun casts first bright rays of dawn
awakening me

sunshine baked juices
from fingertip to elbow
crust a young boy's arm

this warm candle flame
stretching toward the midnight sky
reminds me of you

Battle Cry

back in the days before evil was born
i used to spend my carefree afternoons
roaming the vast garden of earth

but all that changed once the serpent gave birth
to the first acts of definace, and blame

and the people looked down and were ashamed

my restive days and sleepless nights are now and forever filled
by the search for new recruits

wanted:
open minded able bodied freedom fighters

degree in phraseology recommended but not required

slave to the tired and the huddled masses
i enroll millions in mediation classes
and inquire of friends and countrymen alike
to kindly lend me an ear

and i can teach possibilities of joy filled years
turning mortal fear into immortal cheer with just
the flash of my smile

like inspiration to the bastard child i create potential
by spreading visions of a virtuous tomorrow
across disenchanted miles

i helped solomon build an empire
founded on courage and fortified by wisdom
yet pleasures and riches soon led him astray

and still today i seek out articulate potentials
literary mercenaries who can spread my message
to the ends of the planet and back

it was me first who stacked the mortal and marble
founding the academy at athens greece
ensuring that my voice would forever speak peace

when planted in deep and fertile soil
my thoughts bear rich and luscious fruit

and my juices be floatin' down like rain
soakin' into the nappy brains of my people

i am the eternal flame
driving the weary runner on thru the night
when place with might i grasp him tight
tugging him onward and upward
to carry my torch to distant lands

he spreads my fire to every man

where others have fallen he will stand cause in his mind
i be whisperin
i think i can
i think i can
i think i am mighty
therefore
i am

born of nothing but men's minds they cultivate and grow me
and yet i enslave mankind when they fear or don't know me

a pack of chained cave dwellers flock to breed and mate
these, self proclaimed enemies of the enlightened state
populate the legions of my mortal enemies

ignorance
envy
and hate

their undying ability to procreate leads me quickly to make battle
and at the speed that thought travels
i unravel the dreams that plague sleeping poets

they are the drivers of passion pumping stallions
herded into reality's stables

i morphed into metaphor once and they called me aesop's fables

and like a turn table spinning around
my cipher never ceases
as long as sound can shatter
the blissful state of ignorance
into pieces

my master thesis on the power of music
molds masters our of average earthlings
for i am the reason why the caged bird sings

from dusk to the rise of the sun re-born
i am he that brings memories of hope's last dawn

yet still the spawn of pride fight hard and long

so silently i lick the wounds
inflicted upon the many wombs
of my wife
man's written verse

she lost her fighting stance while slamming in a serpent land
in the battle of general bigot's last stand
poetry was severed from the hearts of man
yet just when the art of rhyming threatened to cease and be no more
this new thing called hip-hop armed me with rhymes galore

so i be aimin' my darts at the hearts of youth
with semi-automatic riffles loaded with truth
but don't shoot until you see the whites of their lies
and don't fire if you can feel the self loathing in their eyes

the day that i lack compassion
is the fateful day that my mission dies

i am
the wounded warrior

jaded
yet ever crawling towards peace
and ever searching for restless writers
to set my soul at ease

won't you fight for me

Cycles

to look but never see
to listen but never hear
to seek but never find
stop it
stop it
you're killing me

Blues Traveler

its been a long time
since i've roamed these weary streets
and stopped for conversation
with every bright set of teeth

well, its been a long time
since i've roamed these weary streets
my note book's got cobwebs
from lack of lead to eat

and i got a whole nest full of unpublished ideas
premature hatchling poetry
just waitin' to spread its wings and fly

but first
i got bigger
fish to fry

finding a home that's truly yours is no easy task
now i'm certainly not a lost boy
just a wanderer with a pen

i write down all i hear and see
and my homeboys be givin' me dap
  yo man, dat joint was phat

my professors not their
heads and agree
  exhilirating erudite poetry

but i'm just a wanderer with a pen
it's the question that drives me
question

quest i on
what quest am i on
come over and see

well i got b.b. king problems as i await the a-train
i'm in no hurry

and i can't help
but to think
that the thrill really is gone

as i watch the gloomy shadows of office buildings
that really do scrape the skies

broad is the way of the dollar sign
that created the ruler who measures how high

a pious piper lulling away our dreams
into a scramble for what he calls progress

yeah, the thrill is definitely gone away from me
and now that i'm free from the spell
i can practice improvisation in my own modality

mixo-lydian always did give me trouble

then again i seem to find that no matter where i'm runnin'
but i do think i hear my train-a-comin'
from this lonesome place

i head out west
where i can feel the heat
swell and suffuse inside my chest
where blazing saddles and lifeless canyons
rim the landscape of all i see
temperatures that soar like sizzlin' grease
snap, crackle, and poppin' on my bemused creativity

the heat must be playin' on my mind
puttin' me in a purple haze
i been here 2 hours
and it feels like 99 and one half days

but wait a minute something's wrong here
desert's not as lifeless as it first seemed
the animals give me warmth in the cool of the night

so i join the coyote howlin'
at the moon's black feet
and freestyle with armadillos
who mix all their own beats

taking it all in i sit back and marvel
at my new found community

comm unity   com un ni   come u nite
 come un i fy   come un tie

come untie your minds some more

next i choose to travel down south
not the dirty south
where billie's strange fruit soak each and every tree
but the lush green islands of the caribbean sea
where the sun burns in an altogether different fashion

down here all the lights turn red
all the clocks go dead
there are no norths in the town of the dread

only good vibrations
like a trenchtown dancehall till morning light
i'm rippin' and roarin' thru my bi-coastal mental flight
soarin' round silver lined clouds
till my offspring take flight

this is a place where white clouds
mirror clear blue waters
and a satisfied soul is not a contradiction
but only a deceptive cadence

nature has made clear what harsh realities are really there
like an old marley hit floatin' thru smog soaked air

so let the sun and the moon
and the wind and the stars
and forever erase your fantasy

i could spend forever in each breathtaking dawn
but like the ever flowing sands of time
i gotta keep movin' on

the great lakes of the central states
can ease my mind as well
and i can already tell the reason
why birds fly north for the summer

endless stretches of clear blue lake that don't stop ripplin'
and won't let my soul stop tricklin' out words to my pen

the lyrics seem heaven sent
as i write poetry by moon light
the sun never was quite enough

yeah, its been a long time
since i've roamed these weary streets
like a coltrane turnaround i'm spinning
on the back end of my beat

enjoying my journey
i make the most of every scene
and my progression stays true
no matter what variation on theme

my stones keep on rolling
gently, down the stream
verily i say unto you
life is but a dream

What Makes A Woman More Than Just A Woman

what makes woman more than just a woman

is it the way her shadowed silhouette remains
etched in my mind after just one dance
the outline of gently parted lips
inviting me in with just a touch of demand
and right before our lips meet
i can just make out the lines that flow
down a soft smooth arm
bending to my will
while obeying hers

what makes a woman more than just a woman

is it the way her smile can light up every part of my soul
or the way her laugh can warm me
from my dreads down to my toes
is it the way her hair feels on my shoulder
as she is lulled sleep by my rising falling chest
or the way her heartbeat can find my rhythm
beat as one
and never loose a step

what makes a woman more than just a woman

is it the soft touch of her lips on the back of my neck
that feeling i thought could only be made
by a swaying palm tree
beneath a setting sun
that touch that makes my liver quiver
without one sip of spiced rum
intoxicating love
that spins me
bends me
and brings me back to earth
awakening to those soft warm arms
i feel the thinness of her skirt
the warmth of her body as she gets undressed
the curve of a thigh that demands to be caressed

smell that
that's the scent of a field of roses
budding to greet the rising sum
wild flower and jasmine take human form
as my scorn is driven away by yet another
and yet i am smothered
by the aroma of one more shot at divine connection
our shared stolen moments of surreal expression
lead me to believe that she must be an angel from heaven
or else the devil in disguise
or maybe she's the devil not in disguise
or maybe she's an angel disguised as the devil
tempting me
taunting me
and showing me her way

what makes a woman more that just a woman

when i may never know which one of those she really is
and i don't even care

what makes a woman more than just a woman
when i can taste the beauty of my future on her fingertips

what makes a woman more than just a woman
when i can say she's mine

Harlem Sunset Poem

every autumn evening
just around dinner time
nestled in the neighborhood
where a nickel costs a dime
the setting november sun
trades places with the downtown skyline

there's nothing like harlem sunset in late november

an incandescent changing of the color guard
that never fails to line these sugar coated hills
with shadow as well as light

its flavor is rich and sweet
like a whooping plate full of
sylvia's crispy chicken and waffles
or the freshly brewed iced tea
that washes it down

these lazily stretching rays reflected on my window pane
reflect the blend of colors in harlem
reflect the blend of colors in me

there's nothing like a harlem sunset in late november

a block of maroon rooftops
softly kiss a copper toned cloud
its color is rich and deep
like otis redding spinning a heartfelt line
that seeps into your very pores

and i never mind watching the twilight fade away
while sitting on the dock of any bay
wasting time
wasting time

there's nothing like a harlem sunset in late november

like a slowly dying candle flame
the orange embers blend into
a pale blue palatte
crackling yellowed leaves
line a street so twisting and narrow
that even cab drivers have trouble navigating

where do all the leaves come from
in a neighborhood with such few trees

there's nothing quite like a harlem sunset in late november

Pieces Of A Man

If you know who you are
you will know who your enemy is – Basho

Read the words as if they are someone else's
and you will realize deep inside how much
they are your own. – Rilke

Paint It Grey

picture a student
who speaks with precision
who seems always broke
from trimester tuition
stuff his possessions in a small dorm room
force him to eat cafeteria food
give him an eye for choosing new friends
teach them to study until 6 a.m.
take him to clubs with the latest dances and songs
or smoke filled frat houses that party all night long
give him free time to read books in the sun
and to light scented candles for hitting home runs
have him choose classes by rolling a pair of dice
then remind him that these are the best years of his life

The City So Nice

that they had to keep namin' it
over and over and over again
nyc   nueva york   harlem world   shoalin   brooklyn zoo
the bx   queensbridge   midtown   liberty island
long island   ellis island
and sometimes riker's island

i see a tropical paradise of vibrant livin'
but for the those up to date on the native toungue
it can get wild

especially once i escape
the bright lights and skyscrapers of my
"authentic city tour"

oh, i'm no tourist
this is my home away from home

so rather than sit thru the ever droning stories
of how this building or that building came to be

i choose to venture out on my own
and get away from the gawking thrill seekers
pointing and laughin' at the inhabitants of china town

man,
i hope he gets mugged

so i step from the bus and slowly make my way
thru the rugged sidewalks of this amazon stain forest
where graffiti seems to be a valid way of leaving
your mark on the town
well....
when in rome

it's a concrete jungle
with the ever present sounds of horns blaring
or the mating call of a car alarm stunned by a passing suitor
with an occasional fight breaking out when the owner
appears in rage

well, excuse me sir
i didn't realiaze this was your car i was pissing on

but since i'm not a fighter but a lover of life
i take refuge in the underground tunnels
of public transportation

but the transportation is anything but public
as i sense the silent uneasiness of my tightly packed car

uptown girls who grip their purses
or wall street cornies constantly
pattin' the bulge in their wallets

so i like to play tough and pat the bulge in my jeans
and every now and then stare at one of 'em all crazy
like i'm gonna high jack their peace of mind

but i like the subway

so i usually just chill and let the rhythmic clang clang stride
of the modern day trolley ease my mind
and take me away

the subway gives me time
to sit back and reflect on a day well spent
or maybe to eagerly plan out the long night ahead

oh, i like the subway

it rinses my back of the overbearing track of wasted hours
that used to make up my day

but now my day is wasted no more
as i explore the concrete abyss
of this mortar mesh of sweet and tears

and i look around
and i thank God i'm not in kansas anymore

as i step from the reigns of the iron horse
it's raining on my head

it's pouring down the voice and spirits
of a billion songs, jingles, and ballads
from past, present and future

a wild life symphony that never quits
but only regenerates

as i swing on yellow cab vines from one borough to the next
each stop a brand new species with its very own
tastes, textures, and tactics for survival

it's a freeverse unrehearsed tradition
of mixin' and acting upon
not just dreamin' on
of creating but never placating
these may seem like small differences
but to me it's the line between death and life

no frills, no thrills
just giving what you give best to the world
just doing what you love

and all you have to be
is the person you were created to be
down at city college they call it reciprocity
where only a handful of people know your name
and even less than really care

but by night
under the cover of obscurity
i can prowl and stalk any wild game i choose

if you're lucky it might be you

cause when i pounce
i strike with the full force
of poetry, jazz, and theatre
all rolled into one
depending on which phase the moon is in
on that particular night

the midnight marauders in this neck of the woods
spread well seasoned culture
from shades i never even knew existed

i just got back from a place where individuality
is as common as the wind it rides on

where flavor cruises the lights
from broadway to loisada
and flashes its mona lisa grin

from behind an ancestor's mask
taht has finally molded the face underneath

i just got back from a place so anxious for a new day
that its streets are physically steaming with pressure
and the moistened smoke from a pack of unfiltered passion
slow burning
light and smooth

the city that never sleeps
this place don't ever stop dreamin'
this town don't ever stop fiendin'
for the knowledge that's gained
only thru living and breathing
amid experiences in life and love

and i'm runnin' thru the streets chasin' my dreams like
mowgli chasin' baghera in his final test of manhood
and it feels so good
finally i can run free
run
free

i always thought it was an oxymoron for people like me

you know

a rhetorical figure in which an epigrammatic effect is created
by the conjunction of incongruous or contradictory terms

the run contradicting the free
the free contradicting me

but no more

no more shall i weep
for cool springs of artistic expression
that can quench the sahara thirst
my soul's been jonesin' on for seventeen years

i been crawlin' thru handful after handful
of white dry sands, bleached by years
of mal-practiced freedom of expression

but up there
every un-conformed voice piles high on top the other
stretchin' and reachin' to be a part of something real

and every once in awhile
the art driven avant garde cornerstone
explodes with creativity
and all the stacks fall

its uncharted wilderness
but i can't wait to go back y'all

cause this city is nice

this city is nice

this city is real nice

Moonlight

glowing embers of continuous motion
trapped in the chaos above
steadily riding upon the notion
that *all we need is love*

with entranced wonder i watch and i wait
as signs of peace turn into despair
driven by years of anger and hate
the burden alone is mine to bear

time ceases to exist
space no longer matters
only the blinding mist of bliss
can make the moonlight shatter

To Be 18 in '99

is like an interplanetary blackout
that causes every knee to bow
and every eye to close

a semi-quasi-metaphysical day of reckoning
taking inventory of the last two thousand years

so i'm placing my order
at the drive thru window of the universe
and the lady,
the lady,
the lady behind the counter keeps tapping her fingers
and glaring at me
as if i'm already supposed to know
exactly what it is i want

when i just now realized that i am a poet
                              an artist
                              a man
                              human

i've been trying to live up to
who the world wants me to be for so long
that i've forgotten to examine the person i've become

like i just found a favorite hat i thought was stolen
only to find that it fits the head of the person i used to be

and they keep telling me things like
love means never having to say you're sorry
but that sounds more like war to me

and i keep reading in class that
no man is an island

then why do i feel so alone

so i'm poppin' wheelies down the sidewalks of time
and i can't figure out whether my bike
is too outdated a vehicle to get me down my path
or if its not innovative enough

i keep pedaling thru more and more gears
but i will never pedal fast enough
to run away from myself

its like watching a black and white re-run of history
i almost fooled myself into believing
that it might not really be doomed to repeat

so i've been trying to alter the denoument
instead of just filling in the colors

so i'm counting the patterns in the landscape of my dreams
and its like i'm stuck in the eye of a tornado
a living breathing testament to contradiction

if death and life are polar opposites
then how can i feel so dead inside
yet for the first time feel truly alive

and if chaos and calmness share no similar qualities
then why do i feel so peaceful
when i'm slowly going insane

its like i'm trying to balance
my aspirations on the edge of a cliff
i need to know there's something solid beneath my feet
but i have to throw caution to the wind

and now it feels like i'm chained to two trains
running in different directions
and each steam engine is pumping
red hot ashes into the air
until my lungs are filled
with the pungent smoke of confusion and rage

but this chip on my shoulder keeps
giving me flack about taking it like a man

so i take a deep breath and hold in my hit

i should've stayed invisible
i could've easily given
the world a cold shoulder
and just said
forget about it
i yam what i yam

but back then i couldn't
but back then i couldn't
or rather wouldn't understand

so i'm still holding in my hit
as i await the end of this childhood hangover

and its like watching my spirit regurgitate my soul
as my body rejects the bitter truth

but i suck in more smoke and i hold in that hit
and i hold on to that rage and that confusion
and that confusion and that rage

that rage and that confusion
and that confusion and that rage

so i'm still holding in my hit
as i helplessly sink to the bottom
of the wave pool of reality

and i'm calling out to anyone
or anything that might be listening
to please toss me a life vest

oh God

allah, mohommed, buddha, jesus, moses, confuscious
osiris, isis, zeus and hades, vishnum brahma, jah, jehova

oh God

help this child of yours escape to freedom

Locks

running my long bony fingers
thru these longs thin dreads
i am reminded of the who i used to be
and the man i will become

my roots
and my future

they remind me of my patient dedication to my dreams

they remind me of my inseparable bond
between my family
my woman
and myself

yes, they remind me of myself
my bond with myself
and my own isolated space in the universe

they remind me of a softly setting sun
casting shadows on a cool drinking hole
at dusk

they remind me of children
black children
naked and unashamed
untainted
cloaked in the warm gentle breeze
of a grassy plain

they remind me of music
a calypso hip-so beat
backed by the effortless rhythms
of an easy skankin' singer

they remind me of youth
strong and unaware
boldly and blindly going
where they've never dreamt of

they remind me of the earth
filling my splayed fingers with handful, after handful
of the rich brown soil

locks, i am not ashamed of you

for no matter how many raised eyebrows
no matter how many odd stares
no matter how many up turned noses
or rasta jokes
or failed interviews
i will not forsake you

let them turn their heads in disgust and utter ignorance
let them cast unforgiving glances of spite and repulse

let them stare
let them stare
let them stare

and secretly wish that they too could love you

the way i do

For Her

at night
while i lay in bed

caught between the softly swaying tides of sleep
and the ever surging stream of conscious thought
my gently rocking empty vessel
always seems to drift toward you

that is when i know you best

it is the color of a thousand celestial dawns
a swirling cataclysm of light and darkness
casting an ephemeral gleam on everything in sight

and it smells like spring

i asked you for a simple kiss
instead you showed me your world

for it was you that showed me how to listen to the sea
and together, we blew kisses to the wind
and danced circles 'round the sun
until the radiant glow blackened the vibrant rays
that light up the noon time horizon

and it was good

next time there's a solar eclipse
turn your head toward the sky
that's me and that's you
and that's you and that's me
dancing in a soulful harmony

a harmony of the soul

a spiritual tango
to the allegro tempo
of tito puente drumming in our veins

we danced
and we danced
and we danced

we danced until our bleeding hearts could no longer
stand the hot gusts of air our lungs longed for
or the pounding sound of life blood in our ears

is this the answer

no
its only another question

but rather than quest after answers
to the misty grey ambiguities
that cloud my skies
i have decided to embrace the rain

so excuse me if i come across as over zealous

but the only way i know of
to handle these vernal downpours
is to pitch back my head
squeeze my nose shut
and plunge as deep as i can get
into this oasis of joy
that only gets better
with each consecutive splash

never mind the hazardous undertow
i'm through testing muddy waters

i asked you for a simple kiss
instead you shared your dreams

but this is no fabrication
no trancelike stupor
from which i may awaken
with the snapping of some
distant echoing fingers

nay,
i love you

the way i value sight

the way i take in breath

the way i love life

Meditation No. 2

i start
by noticing the stillness
of my body finally at rest
and i breathe
deeply

i try to keep
my thoughts gently flowing
like a calm and steady stream

instead they are like waves
crashing into one another
each swelling crest eventually
curling over and falling apart
into a thinly scattered layer
of serf and foam

there is a central current
from which these waves are born
i have not found it yet

i continue to breathe
deeply

i can not feel my fingers anymore

before me lies complete
and utter nothingness
void of any describable
physical quality

it sort of reminds me of the construct program
in that movie with lawrence and keanu

i am afraid
for i am truly alone

and yet i know this is the way it has to be
because this is the way it is

although no longer certain
if i am still deeply breathing
i begin to feel magnetized
to separate points
on either side of me

and now i am
stretching, twisting, bending
in opposite directions
that don't necessarily
oppose one another
i do not resist

from some point behind me
i take notice of
or rather am noticed by
a great energy force
something i can not
see or touch or hear
and yet i can not
escape its presence

from some point behind me
a voice more sensed than heard
more felt than understood
enters my space
and all at once
my entire universe
is filled with song

just when i recognize this voice
as being neither internal
nor completely external
to my being
i receive words
to represent thoughts
yet i know they are
a poor imitation

i need to speak with you

the words express
and yet i know
i am the one
who needs it most

but where can i find you

the question
barely takes form in my head
before the answer sounds out
an echo in my mind
even as the words are uttered

in all things

and immediately
i think of at least
57 other questions
i want to ask

instead i find myself
slowly paying heed
to my breathing

the floodgates
of my consciousness
are opened once more

in an outburst
my thoughts
return to me
and i notice
that my foot
has fallen
asleep

An Open Letter To You

if i had but one chance to tell you goodbye
i would say it without ever using the word

i would tell you of long walks headed no where
and longer conversations headed toward the same

i would recall countless moments of you being there
a warm shoulder to sleep on
a soft voice to get me thru the night
or maybe just a constant reminder that
trouble don't last always

i would go on about crowded sidewalks
filled with frantic lives
and how your comforting presence
restores me to self

for i have searched the world over for peace
and found only you

i would try to make you understand
what you have been to me
more than a companion
closer than a mere lover could get
in the midst of the darkness
you have been a light ray
brighter than the starry skies at night
you have forced me into your orbit
i accept

i would tell you that a part of your identity
will remain with me forever
for you have left your fingerprints
indented upon my soul

how many times can two spirits die
and be reborn again
lets find out

and when our paths do cross again
time will yield her forceful hand
restricted expanse will be no more
and we too shall build
another castle in the sky

THE BLACK WHOLE

MILLENNIUM POETRY
BY: JULIAN THOMAS

BOOK TWO:
THE MAELSTROM YEARS

"No one can keep me from my destiny."
-- Stevie Wonder

Introduction:

The number of black holes in the universe may be greater than that of visible stars.

The goal is to create a gravitational energy so strong that all who come in contact will be pulled in.

Infinite density
Zero volume

Focus on the distance to the center, the black tide is what pulls you in.

A black hole has an infinity at its center.
--Fred Alan Wolf

That infinity, is your soul.

Eclipse

"Who says that my poems are poems?
My poems are not poems.
After you know that my poems are not poems
then we can begin to discuss poetry."—Ryokan

Not Now, But Right Now

do it now   do it now   do it now   do it
now   do it now   do it now   now. . .

this is the first day
damn that, this is the first moment of the rest of my life
pulsations and heartaches piling up like fallen autumn leaves
with a dual edged steel rake
and don't let them steal my joy
don'tlet themste almyjo ydon'tl
ethem steal my joy joy joy   do it now
keep searching for new toys   do it now
new ways and reasons to smile   do it now
and let my spirit run free awhile
practice teach learn grow/ will fulfill instill propose/ create demonstrate
relate to acquire/ persist insist build and retire/ proceed fuse bleed mack
hold it down/ rejoice in the world but hear the sounds/ protect inspect rise and go forth/
produce enlighten bow lower than dwarfs/ create create create and set free/ let your
spirit dive to the depths of the sea/ thrive writhe dive and dance/ feel your heart beating
at the hems of your pants/ don't loose sight and don't loose faith and don't loose track/ let
the world fade to black and then fight back/ march on and rally the troops/ find knowledge
of self then kick truth to the youth/ open your eyes feel the light and come clean/ forget
about the facts just become the dream/ bust the seam remain keen/
walk your path but don't forget about your team/ stretch reach seek and listen/ patiently
unwind the mind you been given/ don't worry strive happy/ the goal is near/
it may look hazy now but the outcome will be clear
doitnowdoitnowdoitnowdoitnowdoitnowdoitnow
it was life
and it was love
and it was free
as free as the dream soaked clouds lingering above my head
and it was me   and i can touch them

           in fact i can become them
i can let the rain that is their essence drip-drip down to my outstretched
palms and sing a song for you
     now is all that there is
      now is all that i can give because it's all that i am
      the problem is i think i have time
and what's that voice that keeps calling my name

from just over my left shoulder   this
i turn around
and there's
no one
there
no   here
there is no there
there is only here
but how do i turn
around to myself   now
practice
if you've got nothing to die for
how can you truly call yourself
alive   i'm tired of this immobilizing fear
and the resulting guilt   get over it and do it now
get over it and do it now
the storm will pass but do it now
now is the winter of our discontent but spring is coming   doitnow
my one and only true enemy is myself
for that's the only one that can defeat me   do it now

8/00

Learning How To Get Thru Life Without Living

i used to be a poet
i used to wake up in the middle of the night
plagued by the vivid images in my dreams
and grope in the thick heavy darkness
for an ink pen and a light

i used to spend hour upon gut wrenching hour
flipping thru my 9th edition collegiate dictionary
for just the right connotation or flavor to a word
and i loved it

now
i'm not quite sure what love is anymore
all i'm certain of is that i don't feel it
even from the ones who love me most
especially from them

maybe
maybe somewhere in the dark recesses of my mental playground
there's a set of rusted chain link swings
where me and my inner child can learn to play together

but today is a 'b day
and the rains are keeping us inside
and my inner child isn't any good at checkers
                    10/00

And Justice For All

it never was america to me

that beer battered super sized drive thru window of opportunity
flashing across my screen during the tv timeout commercial break
filling my head with ache after pop cultured aching image
of bob barker claiming he has the right price
to cure my limp financial erection
or the boys in blue asking me what i'm gonna do
to survive their service and courageous protection
a group of pasty green party liberals
pattin' their backs and singing in the rain
and all i wanted to do was finish watching the knicks game

i wish it was america to me

i wish i could stroll thru parks on warm sunny days
wave a tri-colored flag and float on amber waves of grain
i used to spend my firecracker days gazing with wonder
and sometimes i'd even swell up a little with pride
but now the bootleg sparklers that once lit up my eyes
are nothing more than pretty colors dancin' in the midnight sky
sparkling trails of decombusted embers like half dried weeping willows
weeping for the pillages of the past

and i wonder why i never prayed to make my child hood last

as a kid i'd spend that fabled day of independence daymaring about
a la mode apple pies and endangered bald eagles
adorable mickey mouse ears and north atlantic seagulls
but now my night dreams are filled with
jamaican sunsets and freedom flavored watermelons
and krs-one freestylin' with bob marley in the front seat of a '69 caddy

laid back
just ridin
down a one lane highway to heaven

maybe that's the only place i can find the freedom i seek

the american way is closing in on me

four walls of solitary refinement
and from the days of pre-school up to retirement
we ride the education spinning wheel of lies
to get the clay forms of our minds carefully molded
so it don't surprise me that their symbol of justice
is always blind folded

lady liberty
ya blind baby

ya blind to the fact of who i am
so why should i wait for you to listen

i spend enough time wiping the patriotic crust
from my own eyes to maintain 20/20 vision

the act of daily re-creating my dilated irises
has acquired a deficiency by the red
the white and the blue viruses

and i never meant to spread my hollowed out t-cells
to any unsuspecting third world peoples

but mass media done pimped my dreams
for a major motion sequel

grinning and flashing on the big screen just to get famous

bling blingin' my way to the bank as a modern day andy and ammos

prostituted talents of suspect superstars
like premature jism splattered on back seat window

she never was gracious enough to swallow
and too lazy to roll down the glass

and i wonder why they never taught sociology as an acting class

but for the sound of those benjies flippin in my ear
i'm forced to whore my talents for artistic stimulation
sliding my lubridermed heritage across the b.e.t. station
reduced to cultural masturbation

naw she never was america to me

what republicrats want to serve up
as a melting pot of open minded multiculturalism
is like passing off some colored pencil sketches
as a 3 dimensional prism

they don't have the tools for it yet

but still we simmer

and soon we will boil

31 million flavors
condensed into one
bitter
nasty
soup

with no alphabet

and no chunky tomatoes

but the label says democracy so everyone feels fine
and jergens don't make a vida wash to cover up this scent
i need space
i need time

i need to commune with the liberated minds of my past
before we came to this pseudo land of the free

but my ancestral spirit was stolen from me
and whipped into shape with a capital 'c

like an exiled odysseus
sailing eastward hopelessly

like a crumbling sandcastle
floating from sea to shining sea

america you never
were america
to me
                12/00

Poem Almost Wholly in the Manner of Amiri Baraka:No Regrets

i am outside of someone
who loves me. i look
back into her eyes. hear
what rank scents come out
from her voice. hate her
pleasant greetings

cracks in the concrete, for growth. when
my head sits spinning at the warm breath
the sigh of peak, or supple skin
rubbed against me, a magazine, a movie
without smile, or embrace, or fulfillment

it can be fear. (as then, as all her
ambition frightens me) it can be that. or
fear. as when she ran from me into
her service
                or fear, the heart
brown and muddied cast into the
earth, lower than even alter boys
thought Diablo would be
or fear. and the other. the maybe. (inside her thoughts,
her rouge toenails, they are fixed images and were never
free.)

growth, expanding as the fern, the stealthy
virus. a teen ball player in mid season.
or the cold snow in its heap.

cold words flowed thru tense deaf ears. growth,
sinewy, twisting, and tight. stretched as the bubble
with its gum. it is an alien hostility
i live outside. an emaciated hobo
you recognize as beat or simple passion

but it has no passion. as the concrete is stiff
it is not given to tenderness

it strikes that thing
outside it. and that thing
cries   3/01

When I Die

i'd like to see her face again
before i die
a warm beam of sunlight
on the moon's dusty plain
i'd love to see her face again
before i die

when i die
i want to have a number one
carved onto my tombstone
no lofty quotes
no tear ridden roses
just one
cause then i'll be home
where its safe and free

when i die
i want thousands of people
to cram into palladium
and send their cries
to heaven
then jam together in full harmony
then meditate together in full peace
and pieces of the energy wave
will resound like a sonic boom
from one corner of the galaxy
to the other
and all the lonely souls
will be able to hitchhike across
for free

when i die
i'll have my body floated out to sea
viking style
and each of my best friends
will light the straw matted tomb
with one blazing arrow
painted red black and green
and the red white and blue
feathered tips will singe

in the undulating flames
and my family members will each
set one lotus blossom
cascading downstream
one of which will change direction
and fight the current
a stubborn salmon desperado
desperately reaching for a stream
that never was

when i die
i don't want to be remembered for
the books of poems
or the broadway shows
or even that episode on leno
no, i'd rather you remember me thru
the people i've touched
and the friends and family
who knew me best
their lives are a testament to my faith
     11/00

Rainmaker

from this view it seems like the fires may never cease

orange and bright yellow flames
licking and flickering
against a pale grey sky
that's getting darker

yep
from up here
i can see endless stretches of field
overlapping the sunflower forest

that'll go too before dawn

the ignited coals of my written
and verbal bonfire of expression
have plenty of fuel to torch an endless supply
of ideas and questions and passions

that's the easy part
the idealized multidimensional
poet's eye view
of how the world ought to be
how it will be
soon

but that type of flame only gives off
the black ashen smoke that burns the lungs
like tar from firestone tires
and even now the clouds gather with one another
forming layer upon layer of thick heavy ashen air
the cumulus with the nimbus
letting their powers combine
and where is captain planet anyway
he's probably too smart to hang around
in this sweltering grey humidity
but as for me

i choose to get my buckets ready

cause when the rains do come
and i'm told they always do
i gotta be ready to fill my well

until then i dance the jig of the shaman
and dream about home
1/01

Event horizon

"Here I begin to once more treat the same questions about god and the human mind, together with the starting points of the whole of first philosophy, but not in a way that causes me to have any expectation of widespread approval, or large readership. on the contrary, I do not advise anyone to read these things except those who have both the ability and the desire to meditate seriously with me, and to withdraw their minds from the senses, as well as from all prejudices."— Descartes

For Lonely Poets who have Considered Suicide When the Truth Wasn't Enuff

1.
my inner self feeds on the shadows of my
subconscious, a feast that my super
ego can utilize to dine with the divine

but the id in me still hungers

my life, like others has been circumcised by stars
no, not those shining beacons of wonder and delight
westward leading, still proceeding toward an
emaciated ideal glowing brightly in the east
the levitating bar
the internal glass ceiling

as a man i think myself
to be master of the universe
as a poet i know i am

but what would your happiness be had you no public for which to shine

some cat named nietzsche said that
like a hundred years ago
over in europe too
wonder how his
lines can hit me
with so much
truth

2.
day follows day and its contents are added
the new contents themselves are not true
they simply come and are
truth is what we say about them

said william james
but the philosophers are dealing in shades

we who live and breathe know truth
with brutal intimacy

truth, the hand that slowly twists
the jagged dagger into the muscle bound back of atlas
droppin' 30 pieces of poppy seeds on the way home
(a retrospective substance)

the noble nature of the great titan
is steady silence
eyes saddened and alone
veins pulsing and taut
condemned to gaze upon
the harsh realities of the world
from the outside in

3.
the vampire doesn't have to say
the light will kill him
he is already a creature of the night

it is the call of the wild black yonder that now beckons me
the shadow that my soul makes when it has fallen to earth
the part of me illuminated into darkness
an unstill life silhouette of thus and thus

every time i gaze into this non-stop mental mirror
from behind a set of cool dark self mutilated eyes
reflections of my mental state are all that i can see
and yet the cracked lenses are uneven
the sharded pieces scratch and scrape the
thick greasy membranes of my cerebral vortex
get stuck in crevices
plant seeds deeply

its gotta hurt
there's just no other way

4.
the days of my childhood have long since ended/ ended but not forgotten/ i done moved
on/ from rhythmical riffs of emotion and design/ to mutated distortions of thought
and funk/ george calls it da cosmic slop/ a multilayered embryo of impulse and destroyed
desire/ forced into flight before the hatching/ and even if these wings don't never sprout
it ain't gonna keep me from flying/ cause me and brother wind are like a pair of siamese

twins/ separated at the medulla oblong-iforgotta lock the gate on the backyard of my thought patterns/ the unchained melodies have escaped me and continue to run free at this very moment/ they are breeding with stray mixed bred free verse mutts/ the off sprung mongrel aesthetics that will one day find their home in my pad need not fear/ for they can take nothing from me that i would not part withal/ except my pen sir/ except my pen

5.
they raised the price on dreams again
now one must choke and bleed and vomit forth excellence
now one must exceed the boundaries of the skin
just to dance the 2 step
but i gotta tap out savior glover beats
across the hardwood floors of the milky way
and when i look toward the heavens
in search of my constellation
my starry guide
i can't make out the celestial bodies
from those handcrafted flying machines
that now plague our once friendly skies
i never had that problem back home
and i don't wish to defy gravity
i want to become one with it
only then will i truly be able to soar

6.
i accept my fate and await what may come
joyfully
like the gentle brown bear
who snuggles in to his cave for the winter
knowing that spring will come
whether he lives to see it or not
it does come

7.
and when all else fails let the words be a prayer
a holy scripture offered up as sacrament
unleavened

it is the spirit of my spirit that makes it rise
never me, never me

8.
i must become like the shapeless smoke rising from a
single spark of incensed stick: nothing but motion,
impulse, funk, with nothing left to do but spread

no greater power or higher calling or more urgent
matter than to reflect the light until dawn, with hopes
that by morning the people will have found their sunglasses
again

7/01

Zen and Poetry

out of any two thoughts i have
one is devoted to poetry
but i have yet to learn the importance of a line

no conquer pen

as would mountain
when climb
is not mountain also legs
when write
ink and paper control poem
as much as hand

i want to write another book but i can't

i can only write poems
and now it seems even those are falling short
of my relentless search for truth

stop searching

but all i can do is write

then write

discipline in spontaneity
and spontaneity in discipline

its like a gentle swaying
an almost ocean like rocking
against the rhythmic crescents of my disjointed thoughts
joined only by the common constant desire to create

no focus
no control

no patience
no trust

do not try to finish poem
hopeless
only try to realize truth
then u see is not poem that is crafted
but only yrslf

creation is the bridge between me and Allah
zen say stand by yr thoughts as u would a wide river
proverbs say diligent hand will rule
kant say greatest value in world to man
freedom of choice

so if i widen the bridge between
my valuable thoughts
and my diligent hands
what greater world am i free to create

what greater man can u choose to become

i take my tea the way i take my poetry
first thing in the morning
with two bags of earl grey
that have been soaking since last night
sipped with meticulous patience
its almost strong enough

if you do not do the things u love
you will easily forget the joy u found in them

takes plenty faith to put down sail
and float to current
that current shall set u free

but taste of freedom is bittersweet

of this i know too well

i'm searching for that raw uncooked truth
so elemental that it has no composition
only decomposed atoms to its fibers

patience
let the poems right themselves

drugs are a natural thing to mistake it for
but i've tasted what's real

no impulse
no thought

no patience
no truth

him that i felt could do for me is trapped inside
somebody that's slowly killing me
and i didn't even know he was there until now

abuses my use of time
puts poison into my body

he is choking the life from me as we very speak
this person must die a violent and horrible death

no, u must let him slip from the outstretched grasp
of your scarred and hang nailed fingers

slowly and quietly
and stealthily retreat into the night

no open mind
no open eye

no passion
no peace

in order to become a creator i must first create myself
5/01

Memo From the Lawyer I Could've Been

blue sun rising over clear yellow sky
shadows of white that lengthen until noon
expanding sounds of the street life pound my
windowpane: a cacophony of car horns and sirens
and car horns and shouts of fear and dejection
bullets ring out in high school cafeteria
and on the next page a little girl's hand
is blown off by the land mine thought to be
a shiny new fisher-price model
and the half empty whiskey bottle sitting
on my desk doesn't care that it's pushing
my wife away, or scaring my children
all it knows is that it stops my hand from shaking
long enough for me to finish these legal briefs
and at the end of the day
i can walk out of this office
with my head held high

bloodshot as my eyes may be

5/01

30 Hours Before Opening Night of Dutchman

a desk
a pen
silence

need

hugs
kisses
warm embrace

cold death

need

chisel
marble slab
warm rain

moonrise over blue green lake
full and orange

a bowl of kind and 1 match

icy cold chicago wind

fade to black

and teeth marks and bullet holes
and slowly growing circles of red
and slowly dying candle flames

shadow puppets of hiroshima
and mushroom clouds of blunt smoke

the smell of reefer in the air
mixed with day old bed funk
pizza and rum

cracked corona bottles that slice my big toe

hangnails and young screams
young suburban white screams
of fear and loathing
las vegas bulbs shattering

and cracked teeth on cold pavement

and no one notices

and those who do don't care

10/01

Meditation On Meditation
(Poem half in the manner of Charles Wright and half in the manner of myself)

a single moon clear and bright
                            in an unclouded sky
yet still we stumble in this world's darkness

how simple and chaste were the words of the ancients
calligraphic star charts of mystery and sage wisdom
mapping out the middle passage
                            from the square to the circle
                            the chaff to the grain
inspiration poems are the best
not to take anything from those complex ideas
that curve along like a twisted valley carved
from years of weathered toil and erosion
setting the boundaries on our mental tributaries

its the impulsive trips downstream that bring us closer to home
        the next step is always right before the eyes
obscurity
    passion
            brutal honesty
                    that's a good start

---

light is a distinctive wave that does not need a medium
to allow its emission thru space

June sun rises
radiant slumbering giant
slowly awakens

to greet the expanding rainbow
encircling cascade horizon

descent into smog shrouded haze like piercing silence
lingering just west of west
the sound of one hand clapping

there's a quiet tension underlying

the heavy stillness of early summer
typical

terminal 4 at LAX is a bustling anthill of workers and warriors
                        gatherers and guardians

much too busy for me to hear the harmonies of early morning
the mating call of the jaybird rising above downtown tinsel rouge

weddings abounding in the parks
                        folks lined up with traditional servitude
something old
      something new
                  something borrowed
            and something funky

---

sometimes the most refreshing thing in the world can be
to just sit outside in the sun and sweat

rejuvenating elixir of early summer pheromones
that broil the skin to cool down the core

we wear our emotions like the shadows at our feet
ignoring and disbelieving the silent wisdom they contain

pressing and suppressing the proverbial inner voice
wringing the dirty laundry out

neglected impulses stretched taut
like kites shifting from one breeze to another

turning and turning in the midsummer air
the way of the samurai is silent immediacy

---

ikkyu said it best:
writing something to leave behind is another kind of dream
      when i awaken i know that there will be no one to read it

the true master lowers himself into illusion every time he speaks
what is there to be said for the natural born teacher

your genius must remain as hidden as your pending insanity
a cerebral solar flare that eclipses the icy caverns of neptune
runs circles round mantras

shimmering mellow tones of grey luminosity
reach up to the stratosphere and cry freedom
sometimes in silence,
sometimes out loud

the true master lowers himself into illusion every time he speaks
what's there to be said for the natural born teacher

sisyphean griot destined to translate the circumference of pi
 into astronomical units that the people can consume

bring the people together and watch what comes forth

---

its june again
        the sweltering humidity of southern california
clings to you like red and blue lights to a rear view mirror

the lengthening days provide ample time for idleness
the devil's underground thought chop shop

welded scraps of inert musings high jacked before the test run
patched and plated notions
scratched free of the grade school serial digits
the carefree ponderings of the silly old bear

unharnessed cogitations like newly pubescent wilda-beast
untamable and massively self destructive

prisoner of war to my own negative energy
the spiraling gyre caught in retrograde motion

when did my thoughts get so damn complicated
i wish i were pooh

---

another dog day of summer
and here i am face to face
again, with my words
still i wake up blinking in disbelief at my own reflection

groggy and crusted eyelids
hoping to catch a glimpse
             of the latent warrior saint
a dread-less unmasked face stares back at me
recognizable only by the dark abysmal eyes

every time i fall, there's the mirror man
face down on the floor with me
reflecting back a body that used to be my own

all that's left is a withered snakeskin exoskeleton
no bones
             no veins
               just empty brown skin
and two eyes that can't lie try as they might

---

if i could find the spot where truth echoes
i would stand there
and scream

i would let the disjointed shrieks of my nightmares
drown out the apathetic whispers of my day

today i vow to cast off comfort
like a ragged cloak desperately clung to
yet no more fit to protect from the wind

a trojan blankey
enshrouding my potential
in the form of a cold drink
and a warm couch

i always knew the answers would only bring more questions
but i never felt the cold futility that comes along with it
                                        until now

i ask myself why the person i want to be
does not shape and mold my inner most desires
i ask myself why the skyscraping dreams of my tomorrows
do not pour their concrete mold
into the muddied out footsteps of my now

california sunshine
      like golden hershey's kiss
just before dawn

when the night time horizon is at its blackest
just when i need it the most

what is it about the unearthly hours between midnight and 5 am
that seem to get the creative juices flowing
maybe it's the fact that they are so unearthly

waxing gibbous moon
      reflected in backyard jacuzzi
in the cool of the evening

i write to liberate my mind from reality
if only for a brief moment
and smoke black and mild roaches when no poems come to mind
      yes, its come to that
      but this only blunts the pain
      and we all know a blunt edge will kill you just as well
          more slowly, but just as well

i thought teen angst was supposed to stop
when you passed from the age group

i also thought true creation was supposed to be effortless
like, god snapped her fingers and the universe exploded
time and space began
or at least came into existence

---

another hazy 78-degree afternoon
life goes on, as it always does

body surfers catch their foamy waves
round eyed kids build beachside castles

just near the water late day sun sparkles in the salt stiffened sand

me, i need only one grain to set my mind back to the task
of contemplating the expanses of the universe

the mental state of my joyful solitude blows freely like the wind
      deeply like the earth

                    and passionately
          like the rays of the sun
from the whisperings of the grass to the heartbeat of the trees
i am one with time

lonely only when i have no one with which to share
the beauties of the cosmos

like the ocean's symphony of sound
crashing in, fading out, and crashing in again
rainbow tinted eyelids that shield from amber brilliance

reflected vibrations from the giver of life
sending their praises skyward
          along with everything that has breath

---

situation can never be an excuse for not being free
is it my contentment with life that ensures my inner freedom
no that's an effect, not a cause

descartes was only half right
there is no thought without a subsequent action

no matter how quickly i progress i feel no centrifugal velocity
only a force pulling inward
                    a finely tuned reverse telescope
peering into darkness thru the incorporeal gravitational lens

light from the horizon of events changes everyone's color frequency
          some shifted red
            some shifted blue

the impermanence of the world is only the beginning

je pense donc que je suis
          non, je danse donc que je suis

(i think therefore i am
  no, i dance therefore i am)

                              8/01

THE BLACK TIDE

"If I don't die today I'm gonna try to change the world."
-- Bone Thugs n' Harmony

Original Man

on the eve of the last great celestial war
the children of Zion gather in the fields
of their ancestors' memories

they hang their boots in the trees along with their minds
that they may feel damp grass on the softened souls
of their bare feet one last time

time

time
i need more time
time to let my light shine round

illumination that penetrates whether candle or mirror
i'm gazin' into blackness but my reflection's gettin' clearer
i steal degrees from ivy leagues while shadowboxin Uncle Sam

i am original man

ignitin' crowds with the inner strength of Shabazz
scribblin' dreams of tomorrow over promises past
the cool gaze of bhudda and the ghetto stroll of shaft

brighten your vision like a sun ray
we gettin paid
spoken word is like wildfire
with guns and berets

and black fists with black gloves
that fought hatred with black love
we send doves cross the sea
clutchin' cotton to show peace
but our brothers in the east
say that we marked with tbe beast
naw, forget whatchu heard
had enough pasty words
if you're scared, or unsure
just retreat to tbe burbs

twisted offa this world of sin
but the only way we survive

is to strive to become gods instead of men
is it the evil that men do or the evil doin' man
its hard to live proper when your existence is a scam

blood coursing thru my veins with the passion of sonny liston
gave up on feeding my brain when i ain't have a pot to piss in
bending the light to set things right
illuminating these ghetto prisms
these primordial jisms
how do i cross a schism most people can't see

seminally blinded
took it back to the days when i was criminally minded
oh wait, that day didn't never cease
and i can't take credit its a gift thru my teeth
drawin' chalk outlines in the imaginations of the past
raising verbal pyramids whose apex might last

i blow tunes that heal wombs and impregnate the sea
my syllogism spreads life like the birds and the bees
lyrically you wanna perform armed robbery
but i slapped another wack mc
before he could turn his back to me
man, you talkin' bout auto rhyme tasers?
to mythological minds i am still the dragon slayer
and into blocks i chop the knowledge of the sea
my color-coded building blocks of creativity
soakin' the rubex cubes into my breakfast tea
the tea that gives me lunar energy

born under the 7th moon of taurus
mental etch-n-sketches are deeper
than the hieroglyphics of horus
i make pencils out of redwood forests

pile 2 scoops of rebellion on my slices of the doomsday pie
20 seconds on the mike and not a panty in the room stay dry
but my dollars stack swiftly and kiss lucy in the sky

call me a literary master p
forget that, i'm a zulu chief
crossin' legislative mountains
with the resurrected elephants of hannibal
muchin' on their quotas with the vigor of a cannibal
striving to fuse my blackness with that eternal blue sea
and they killed huey so what you think they gonna do to me
even in death i got a hot comb to their karma like an afro-deity

whether formed as the tao-te ching or a streetwise magazine
i see respect in their eyes but rarely understanding

too many wannabe revolutionaries tryin' to battle me
but they logic is too full of cultural fallacies
too many fake ass reactionaries slippin' thru the seams
too many grown men stuck in peter pan dreams
oh, there's a never never land waiting for you
where you can gang bang forever with no plan or pension
and lust after fairies in the cellblocks of san quentin

think of all the joy you'll find
when we leave that ghetto mentality behind

i'm tired of watchin' my brothers waste their lives
and lettin' warner brothers depict them
our soldiers are strong but have spent too long
pumpin' fist and fryin' chicken

i be the last of the rhythmic mohicans
beacon shinin' bright but shiploads can't quite see clear

screamin' for justice at the top of my lungs
but it's the whispers that they hear

1,440 chosen to refill zion's purses
1,440 crystal white horses

all ridin' into the sunrise with a newly awakened eye
and each one beggin' for their spot on the front line
gave me enough time to reclaim the wisdom of the serenghetti
when the day breaks the struggle continues
will you be ready

at dawn the struggle continues
brothers, will you be ready

11/01

Lyrical Miscegenation

this is a poem that some of y'all goin' have to understand
(emphasis on the some)

ahhhhhhhhhhhhhhh

cause sometimes ya just gotta scream
sometimes the playing field itself must be tackled
sometimes to get to freedom you gotta tighten up those shackles

have you ever cried out from the edge of a canyon
with hopes that maybe, just maybe
this time your echoing voice won't come back

me neither

i vowed to marry the wisdom of my soul
to imagery and metaphor
a trochaic matrimony tying the knot between
the passion that burns me
and the ink that fills my veins
do you
self proclaimed scribe of the stars
verbal musician extraordinaire
promise to take Whitman and Williams
as your lawful wedded wife
to let Shakespeare be your sugar daddy
in sickness and in health
as long as you both shall live
till death do you part

you gave an emphatic "i do"
so we jumped the broom
and now i have answers
that have raised a completely
different set of questions

what makes a poet the type of poet
that's taught in textbooks
100 years after he dies
is it the amount of change he creates
or the numbers of books he publishes
i fear for the latter

mistrust makes me apprehensive
for the enjoyment of my love
and i know experience is no infallible guide
20 years deep and i have nothing else to lead me
this so-called urban voice
laced with traces of duke's elegance
always seems to fall on deaf ears
i strive to find my vocal precision
in a language that ain't my own
a rich verbal tradition that no matter how
comfortable i grow accustomed to
remains destined to capture only the shadowed outlines
of the thoughts i so desperately long to express

do i love you
or do i lust after your gentle touch
that inspired spark of passion
where all the jumbled phrases
start to make sense
that moment that leaves me blissfully attracted
like a ravenous moth to the very flame
that will one day singe his wings

love makes expectations soar thru the roof
though the applause boosted my emaciated ego
your flame may keep me from ever flying again

its funny how we can repeat an illusion so many times
until we ourselves mistake it for reality

and on the slim chance of love's recovery
i returned to you
with hopes of deepening our affections
only to find that you've moved on to the next new thing

no, i do not blame you for continuing your search of
emotional stability and public acceptance
we're all searching for something
if i could, i would do the same

but that doesn't make your untimely departure
rest any easier with my newly vacated spirit
your spot will be difficult to replace

even though your words never lied
the eyes only told half-truths

it was everything i ever wanted
but it wasn't real

painting a landscape in my heart
with rose stem thorns dipped in lead based paint

green sky, blue moon, yellow river, black sun

i now understand the truth in the statement
that what does not kill can only strengthen
the will to survive

but that doesn't make my nights go by any more smoothly

i suppose i should thank you for that

love always did mean growth to me
more than a man when we were conjoined
how is it that i am less than what i used to be
without you

i almost wish you didn't love me anymore
rather than that you've forgotten how to show it

all i ever wanted was to care for you
and for that to be enough
but change is the only constancy
this life will ever bring
 and if i truly understood that
why would i keep trying to go back
to the way we were

the way we were

a wise woman once said
freedom is another word for having nothing left to loose
well....i certainly feel free
yet still helplessly bound to a truth
that isn't my own

too bad they don't give out the pulitzer for rawness

was i too threatening for the pasty new age literati
too robust for the expressed written consent

of the borders open mic session
if it incites any possible tension
i get patted on the head
and awarded honorable mention
well...isn't that nice

but its all good
cause i never wanted to process my notepad anyway
picture me with a platinum blonde attachment to my pen cap
ink tubes be filled with konkalene cream
poems be fried died and laid to the side
and i be like...yeah right

i don't need no tim hardaway crossover exposure
that'll ensure me a spot on their list of best sellers
a sambo shuffle with grins and flashes
panhandlin' for food that won't satisfy the masses
instead i torch bridges and blaze fires in the ashes
these are the only flames that can defrost my dreams
the ties that bind a quick fix money makin' scheme
are woven with false bandages
more see thru than muslims eatin' pork chop sandwiches
turnin' my back to loose-leaf paper thin deals
marks the dawn of my quest to chase after wind meals
and to think, i used to chase after women
or worse yet, literary recognition
in these strange days its almost a given
that such a frivolous mission
will kill my all-natural artistic high
and for some strange reason
they keep on passing me by
hardly noticing the verbal graffiti
that rims the alleyways
of their urine soaked minds
make me feel like i'm existin'
in the wrong frame of mind
the wrong frame of time
but i'm just jammin' to a slightly different beat
keepin' it real i take my efforts to the streets
grab my grey suede timbs
locate my man o steel briefs
zip up my stonewashed f.u.b.u. jeans
and pretend like this one night stand
really meant nothing to me

1/02

Sestina in Blue
a.k.a. Rainmaker #2

back in the time when there wasn't nothin' but the beat
before shootin' dice, sippin' forties in the street, space
was the final frontier yet to be known. but fear of the black
ness still kept enlightened ones at home. first cracks of rain
and thunder give new birth. wide and wet and cold for earth
bound friends. it all depends on if they love it. inhabit the sky
instead of reachin' up above it. redefine the nursery rhyme
s instead of cursing the young minds, there may be enuff time
to strengthen the frail spines, turn those candles into star
s, whose light exceeds the speed and density of mars. the fire
consumed turned mountains into craters by the light of the moon
master plan of the creator with a little voodoo, call it the blue

s, sad raggy tunes, nothin' to loose, dispossessed from earth
from the very beginnin'. burnin' trees smokin' lucys in the sky
since the mortal sinning, they told me i could be a star
one day like john lennon, or john maybe wayne, just beat
the pain and keep a smile on my face, and keep enough space
between me and the boss's daughter, baby reflectin' the black
ring of the bath water. so now i'm out into the cold ass rain,
ain't never begged for change, we bust caps in the moon
light, hustlin' thangs, seem like i can never do right. fire
in the trash but no heat. my fingers are stiff and blue
from livin' on the street. but still i conduct the rhyme
circles on the ave, and hope i live a long enough time

to take the haves and the have nots, and shorten the space
between, and maybe add a little bit of hope into the black
dreams. awakening the magic people, shines and blinds, fire
ry lines, have a good time, secrets of the brown earth
planted deep in the spine, infinite like a strip of the sky
immediate like a blink of the eye, givin' dap to a star
on the rise, when he stumble folks is lowerin' eyes, beat
in' on him like a pimp on a corner with a 70's rhyme
all balls but no mind, he think he stay true, but the blue
suede pair of his wing tip shoes will keep him strollin' in time
got his honeys lined up on call, plus his cash flow is rain
in' like seattle in fall. dilated shine like the new moon

shit i had been thru, not new to me but usually the sky
above my head's brighter than a sonic boom, a star
ry night that sparkles light from that eternal blue
hopin' you see it too, hollerin' at the wide cold space
keep me shiverin', but my tongue's deliverin' birthrights on black
nights but nobody is listenin', now i see how a fast a fire
blast can steal your glistenin', one day the whole wide earth
gon' know my pain, i'm like a world series game 7 called for rain
anti climactic life but no shame, slappin' fives with father time
because he never complains, just maintains his cycle like the moon
goin' thru changes, we about the strangest, sharing one heart beat
but streets is gettin' dangerous, make 'em believe that their rhyme

is your rhyme, step into your own time, greet the morning star
everywhere you are, fires in you, their rain can never consume
only the bluest eye can penetrate the light of your moon, spirits black
er than deep space nine, we beat the old school minds who never cared,
the earth is our turf so let 'em stare, only the sky above us do we share

10/01

Paradigm Shift

Reality is terribly superior to all history,
to all fable, to all divinity, to all surreality—Antonin Artuad

The Rebirth Of The Cool

in the beginning god created the funk and the cool
now, the coolness was chaotic and without form
and discord covered the face of the deep

and god said
let there be peace

sparkling like diamond
gentle as the ray of the sun
an interstellar drum
with a cosmic heartbeat

and yes, there was the blues

that blacker than 1,000 midnights blue
eternal blazon of endless nothing
that chasm between reason and dream
the place i call home

and the cool was with me
the cool was in me
the cool was me

the cool knew me
the way i know
my very own name

sweeter than the taste of fresh cut sugar cane
we walked the yellow brick paths
of each and every dimensional plane

i sing a song for the cool

that melodic thumping in my ears drums
that comforts me just before i fall asleep at night
the gentle tap taps on the outskirts of my slumber
that whisper sweet nothings of peace and light

i sing a song for the cool

boogalooing jazz hall droplets of sweat
that glisten on brows of every color men
the mutated mind emissions
of castrated time transmissions
searching for a light wave
a loose-leaf page
and a pen

i sing a song for the cool

a post-modern influx
where faith is a crutch
hobbling thru fears of the day

our passions grow slender
but children remember
life is what unfolds along the way

syncopated sound waves
that sparkle like a moon ray
seeking out river bank reflection

resonant and free
we struggle not to be
sissified by delusive introspection

before there was ever any such thing as a wino or a crack head
we were cool

before there was ever any such thing as homelessness or aids
we were cool

before there was ever any single parent homes or halfway houses
or so-called holy wars
we were cool

me, i sing a song for the cool

1/02

Meditation on Morning Prayer

cold dew on damp grass
reminds me to sit at my place in the sun
a little more naked than i was the day before
yet the cloaking winds have picked up
even with the first blush of light

returning to the horizon just after dawn
a crescent moon lingers in the hazy violet sky
just to catch a glimpse of the golden rays
that allow him to shine
sleep well my beautiful moon
your work is yet to come   9/01

Cosmological Shadowboxin'

poems like these ain't real
'less they shine like a chromed out platinum wheel
sun roof open when i roll in my car
so i can drive and look at the exploding stars
white dwarf or red giant it ain't burnin' me
because my comfort zone is wider than eternity
in the club brothers givin' me pounds
but they don't understand the agenda is now
progression is steady like the dreads be lockin'
and i'm cosmologically shadowboxin'
i speak softer than the rain
and as long as i'm a poet imma train
to just listen
to the wisdom of the trees
sweet rustling of leaves
my mental jet skis ride waves of reality
hoppin' on foam, playin' with gravity
but i hold on to the muse when i got her
same moon reflected in every pool of water
i bounce a shine off the liquid for fun
i'm quick as a gun
but i am no sun
the twinkle in your ear caught the way my words gleam
cleaning the mirror every day for a high beam
of is it an illusion
cause god is a verb and its deeper than institution
live for the infinite, forget all else
but maybe i'm gettin' too ahead of myself
first grow wings for arms
or become a wide river mighty and strong
or just quiet down all thought
the cosmos has a rhythm and that beat don't stop
so how you gonna tell me if a tree hits the ground
that it don't make a sound
never mattered
if no one hears
its breakin' up the solitude
and chasin' the fears
cause silence is a weapon
and the sound must rise to the heavens

diggin' deeper roots for the fruits i grow
and there is an edge, this must i know
but i'm done chasin' yesterday with scorn
cause now i see that emptiness if form
and every form is empty
livin' in my nappy now
till i always see everything
collectin' on taxes is wastin' my time
i'm hoppin' synapses of universal mind
stackin' up ladders cause my rise ain't stoppin'
till the day i'm erased into shadows
and forgotten

5/01

Cracked Leaf in Black Sky

spiral flight at dawn
sun bleached locks, sandy brown skin
 awe struck lover gapes

         brown skin lady soars
  thru clear reflections of blue
knees cocked, hair gold, free

 frostbite in daylight
          deceptive shine grins and lies
chicago in may

          shortstop tags runner
          playground kickball, midday sun
          dust settles loosely

water droplets in
          late day sun glimmer in gold
            impregnate the earth

 soft lips feed male ego
                what sweet lies lie behind
            hazel eyes that smile

          orange glow fades quick
 behind pale blue mountaintop
                nightfalls, black like me

cracked leaf in black sky
 sagging branches sway in wind
gathering of crows

 i move in silence
my pen flies like mountain wind
poet samurai

Spring Tundra of North Chi

spring tundra of north chi
flowers bloom
and freeze
and die

ducks confused
back for the summer
too frosty for mating yet
too fogged out to sing the blues

Chicago, where the April showers
fall in ice storms

the streets are cold
the life is harsh
the night goes on
                            4/02

Black Love

black love is tough
the whispered voices of your brown brothers urging you on and keeping you sane
black love is the embrace of your mother as she rocks you gently thru the cold wet rain and
lets you know its goin' be alright
black love is a vicious bark turned into a vicious bite
black love is tough
patiently awaiting the day of parole
black love is keeping a candle in the window
the silent prayers of vacant stomachs trusting the lord
turning their dreams into store bought wishes for a brighter tomorrow
and a satisfied today
black love is that forgotten dream steadily floating away
it shadows the hunger and shines down on pride
igniting the spirit and blinding the eyes
black love is the blues and john coltrane
wailing a soulful tune from the depths of his divinity
spinning a web of castrated desire to set his captive spirit free
the heat of a blue flame on a bright red rose
black love is respect for the lives of the old
blaring confidence and silent despair
the black fist on the back of the comb in your hair
black love is painful
black love is real
the coal in the engine
and the spokes on the wheel
the smoke in the sky
and the stiff iron track
the gleam in your eye
and the sweat on your back
black love is alive, passionate, and free
a single tear drop that longs to be a wave in the sea
black love is 1,000 fists raised high in the sky
a unified voice and a unified cry
black love is the kiss that cools the burn on your forehead
when hot comb meets nap
spicy chicken wings that make you jump back
round brown shoulders glistening in the sun
black love is crazy
black love is fun
black love is everything

the dark side of the moon
the interstellar womb
the cocoon of man's civilization
black love is the spirit of every nation
hand writ sanskrit prayers from ancient kemit
beyond the horizon of the cosmic black sea
the rhythm in you and the rhythm in me
a disregard for the rules, chaotic and free
the beauty in you and the beauty in me
black america is the paradigm twice shifted
black love is the infinite
yes, black love is infinite

7/02

1

heartbeat
heartbeat   and   rhythm
heartbeat   rhythm   and   connection
and   one   moment
that   hopefully   will   never   be   forgotten
                                                            9/02

Then He Told Me I Was Confused About Religion

then he told me i was confused about religion, i
felt the pain of loosing my pure and youthful vision, my
moon was set to mirror the blues of heaven rhythm, but
then he told me i was confused about religion

silence is the mark of my grayish mental countryside,
lining up horizon line to the beat of ocean tide
layering my consciousness while the clouded thoughts roll by
solitary quietude like the mystic mountainside

earth is like the river and man is like the foamy sea
one becomes the giver, the other is the lonely key
locking our existence, a ritual abandoning.
loosing hope of ending the spiritual panhandling

one day i will inhale the smell of heaven's harmony
letting go the physical, oh how much i long to be
drinking from the chalice, the thought it makes me salivate
letting go of malice and jealousy, they're hard to break

out of when the hunger is soaking up my every need,
as i walk alone every blade of grass is cutting me
so i pick up lessons as supple as the willow tree
reaching for the strength of my mother, she created me

in a painful fashion, my passion was a starting line
idolized my mother's security and almond eyes
then i took up fasting for balance and for clarity
see the rain outlasting the darkness that was scaring me

then he told me i was confused about religion, i
felt the pain of loosing my pure and youthful vision, my
moon was set to mirror the blues of heaven's rhythm, but
then he told me i was confused about religion

reaching for the sun was like akeldama drenched in rain
i know what it is to feel built karma lynched in vain
nobody but daniel knew truly how to mold the pain
till you had a handle on growing lilies on your grave

eighty five are cattle, their spirits are like currency
i was born to battle the whipping of the learning tree
fear becomes the teacher with institution governing
me and faith got deeper cause we are one in suffering

blinded by my prideful and egoistic wondering
when i would inspire a movement from the stumbling
i could not foresee, only hear the thunder rumbling
then i saw my purpose and down the wall came tumbling

then he told i was confused about religion, i
felt the pain of loosing my pure and youthful vision, my
moon was sent to mirror the blues of heaven rhythm, but
then he told me i was confused about religion.

holy was the moment i heard the river, finally
surfing on a sliver i felt the current timing me
picking up the pace was like shaking off a diamond ring
almost went to waste but now pearly gates are eyeing me

meditated life in the garden of jetavena
hidden from the strife i submitted to the balance of
sharpening my vision, and i am not the only dove
going unto him as the wheel behind the lonely hub

once i lost my mask, i could feel the burden lightening
moving from the known, to the impulsive enlightening
heated up my lava flow toward the glory of the sea
breaking bread with love just to soar above repugnancy

then he told me i was confused about religion, i
felt the pain of loosing my pure and youthful vision, my
moon was set to mirror the blues of heaven's rhythm, and
then he told me i was confused about religion.

journey toward the center beset by love and faithfulness
self control was mentor, and ohm became the radius
kindly stopped debating the good or bad, now patience is
peacefully awaiting the joy of inner gentleness

every eye was closed, i perceived i had a blessing due
cloud was burning gold and the sky it turned electric blue
buzz inside my ear, but the sound i heard was hallelue
resurrected spirit said 'son, i am anointing you'

live inside the energy to return to innocence
free from all desire your cycle will begin again
let your spirit dance in a manner wholly different
then you will enhance understanding of the infinite

when the spirit vanished it took away the sourness
somehow it had managed to wash away the cowardice
sweeter than the pollen of early april flower, its
strengthening the fallen. the source of all my power is

warm as summer rain, and then in the name of Jesus i
grew a lion's mane, and then in the name of Jesus i
rose above the pain, and then in the name of Jesus, i
found my arrow's aim, and its in the name of Jesus

3/03

The War Poem

aftermath of destruction sparks newfound discernment
hear the wind blow thru the treetops, and the north star is burning

in the streets the paper chase has lowered a veil
and each nation is keeping its greatest leaders in jail

what a time to return, resurrected in the sand
tarnish the name of freedom to exercise my plan

the ballot is a shackle, a leader without a fan
a legal lynching is swung by the executive branch

see, i was born from out the belly of the sweat from the field
brotherhood was the bond that his jealousy killed

the sword kept my hunger supreme, gun powder snuck from the east
destruct the present in the air that you breathe

i wrote the topic when they chopped the map of africa's shores
slayed the natives with the syphilis of european whores

camouflaged in the likeness of truth, a guillotine is my tooth
nuked japan, and almost wiped out the jews

took up the tactics of gorillas when the jungle was lost
i brought the thunder to the desert bombing churches and mosques

innocent lives were taken the banner is steeping clear
they'll never understand my greatest weapon is fear

some say the 7th seal will open like the flash of a gun
they tell me love can not be stolen but i'll blast it and run

re-mastered the plunge, free falling like addicts for fun
i'll make a ruthless paratrooper out your first born son

fresh outta graduation aiming at that first million
a twisted capsule shot the shrapnel thru his grill and was done

took his eyes from the hairs of the cross in hesitation
the moment was lost and now his lungs are suffocating

grasping the finger of a friend from class, he collapsed to the grass
and i just sat back and laughed

squadrons are armed with a vengeful force
see the comrades carving out a lion's war

thought he had the game won, caught him with a flame gun
my name up out your mouth, and we'll keep this shit the same son

label me a psycho, travel as the night blows
tattoo on my chest is an automatic rifle

veterans will die slow, money is my cycle
took my overhead just to fund the spread of white blow

governments been using me, genocide ain't new to me
young people stay high, then go be all that you could be

unemployed recruitment, that's how i get you sent
from the liquor store, now you scrubbing floors at boot camp

mind control is dominant, allegiance i want all of it
took religions hand, now we forming a conglomerate

terror brought me prominence, tragic like the towers that fall
keep your greatest enemy the closest of all

i set the court for black crime, that's how i attack minds
send them overseas, now that's fifty niggas flat line

realize, victory or death the world is mine
its like a jungle sometimes

6/03

I.E.H

True art seems unsophisticated.
True love seems indifferent.
True knowledge seems child like.
True words seem paradoxical.
                    ---Lao Tzu

okay
all the time   now
be present   be aware   be focused   be now

silence
until
the impulse
to speak
            violence
fulfills
        the impulse
        toward heat

autumn bleeds thru gaping teeth on all hallow's eve
and still they call it mysticism
        gentle spirituality's psychedelic evil twin
        devouring mother earth's rites of passages
        one communal toke at a time

as for me, i need a new drug

one that don't lubricate my mind
one that won't silence the shrill voice of conscience
                    with ethical vicadin
                    and cultural novacain

i need a new drug

one that perpetuates its own atomic charge
and jams to the beat of the funk of the stars
whose ego grows thinner when clarity flies in
welcome to the inner event horizon

---

intuition is the mentor of pure genius
            the arrowhead of civilization
forged from the blue steel of things unseen
            the rod and the shaft of creation

training and chiseling from the bottom up
promethean spark re-hydrates man's potential
stone on flat jutted stone

orgiastic dragon eases thru crystal clear sky
       see how he trickles in the wind

bite hard into self-indulgence
       but don't swallow it down
the shadow of the shadow is what spews forth climactic resolve

the inner path is a hall of mirrors
retract the impulse
and set it free
brainwave flutters in a guttural plea
       chew slowly, but don't swallow it down

harmony is the tuning fork of innovation
Stevie Wonder knew this
as did Mozart
the key to perfect pitch is finding the right wavelength
the 12-year-old genius with a golden harmonica
       and there was joy in the morning

---

mondays are for fasting
god's lackluster warm up for the satiated week
how noble is the paragon of pure faith
how polished and glittering his loosened belt buckle
better to repose oneself to the quiet solitude
of meditative hunger
let the congregation applaud their vicarious role models
i choose the dull and steady percussion of humdrum
humility

---

be grateful
especially when you yourself deserve thanks

be honest
especially when you yourself are deceived

be gentle
especially when treated with callous

be respectful
especially when treated with contempt

be tolerant
especially when you yourself are unaccepted

but most of all
be full of love
especially to all those who hate

---

a mirror has no memory

hollowed out echo rebounds the changing face of now
no wiring feedback
no static reverb

the omnipresent looking glass shines moment to moment
in stereo surround
        brilliant vividness by day
        glistened lucidity by night

 the only lens alice ever stepped thru
was the pane inside her own mind
retract the impulse, and set it free

---

fame is just another form of suicide
a free form cobblestone driveway
scrubbed clean of all creative depth perception
        flash photosynthetic sparkle
                            keeps egocentric v6
               revved to the red line
but this garage door is heavy
and i've lost my push button opener

exhausted windpipe leaks odorous gas
the life of the stars is nearly upon me

the carbon monoxide catch phrases
offer slow suffocation of the soul

        jim morrison told only half the truth
                break on thru to the other side
        because even in death
        the struggle continues
in fact, it picks up the pace

undeserving accolades devour the righteousness of man
and thereby consume his immortality
that is the point where nothingness becomes the only absolute
still the snow will fall, and still the sun will shine

and yes, still the dreams of the masses will cloud
the dawn of their leaders

must i forever repent for the sins of my wayward youth
the dizzying sojourn of unquenched desire
an aimless arrow
          sailing thru a cloudless sun scorched sky

the israelites
wandered the desert 40 years
before God brought them home
wonder how long it'll take me

in the meantime
hype crowds, high fives, and the microphone
are a point of reference in the wasteland
          dazzling array of rhythm and reason
          strengthened with every bobbin' head
           a razor sharp cutting edge
           shined to a piercing reflection

          parabolic poetry like the icy
          blue vein rivulets in my arm

          public prominence like the cool
          touch of steel to their pulsing stream

but these powers are not my own
so i give thanks for the breath of life
and constantly strive to dig deeper

strike a sense of fashion
with each star studded nail
pounded into splintered wooden gallows

style is crafted one rejection at a time
and a picture perfect image is a noose around the neck
 shave another five pounds and come back in a week
 fifty pushups in the morning
                    plenty water
                              but don't eat

starved out conviction swings just fast enough
to keep my bluff believable, so the rope won't break
it just swings, and swings . . .

how does the moon ride high enough
      to throw back the break of day

even as the very selfsame sun
hides its lunar face

start with the silence
      that is the longing for the center

eternal stimulation is a self-generated process
and mental spelunking is a full time job
the steadfast polishing of greatness
is no longer an achievement
it is a way of life

the chaos of creation can not be chartered the night before
discovery begins when the whistle is blown
                          like true love
                          like jazz
and when its all said and done
this millennium will mark the dawn of something greater
Father Time's dusty record tablets revamping the cosmic
groove chart of what goes down

it continues to go down
even as we speak

---

today i stood in the smothering shower of late april rain
and gave a blessing to the sky

i let the water soak into my lengthening locks,
already heavy with the downpour of the day
 whose roots are my mother's skin

soaked to the hair of my goateed chin
i paused to feel the beaded wetness dribble from my face
to the black leather coat that wasn't keeping me warm
                        and didn't need to
the fire has returned
what is the feeling of a thousand candles in full array
pulsing their flame to the meter of a poet's vein
 or awakening to the face of your one true love
  over, and over, and over again
      or the holy spirit's rapturous electroshock grasp
      heightening insight to strip down the mask

today i stood in the smothering shower of late april rain
and gave a blessing to the sky

chaotic climate of the modern age
over shadow's the mind's eye
                              and still, like dust, i rise
words are worthless if their light doesn't shine

but they can't resurrect brown bodies laid to waste
and they can't break bread for the homeless or the poor
they can't shelter the battered or the raped
and they can't stop imperialistic war

this nation is run like a spiritual morgue
so i don't have to question what i'm writing for

the enemy comes to distract and destroy
but i don't have to question what i'm writing for

i'm almost a graduate and almost unemployed
still, i don't have to question what i'm writing for

the fire has returned to ignite my inner core
and i don't have to question what i'm writing for

---

hold fast to all that edifies
especially in the mist of sensory appeal

hold fast to all that is humbling
especially in the mist of self-glorification

hold fast to all that is simple
especially in the face of complexity

hold fast to all that is charitable
especially when given wealth

hold fast to all child-like innocence
especially when given power

but most of all
hold fast to all that is joyous
especially when life is a burden of grief

---

the early breeze before dawn is the keeper of secrets
the slumbering playmate of grandfather night
she whispers a dream as she talks in her sleep, listen:

veil of dust
haze of fire
cloud ascension
never tire
stellar birth
oval flare
solar mirror
the eye is there
might of the mind
complex as the stars
endless potential
in black and white bars

my high school buddy is stationed in Egypt
where queens and pharaohs once reigned

they say its different when its someone you know
i tell them its different when its you

living in shadows
sleeping on your feet
feeding on hunger itself

there's more than one war going on right now
in fact, they number the sand on the shore of the sea

neither body nor consciousness
the enemy lies within

there are no P.O.W.s
and certainly no civilians

tunnel vision
blinding pride
refugee compound
millions hide
fallen faith
sparks the brain
heavenly science
nuclear rain
seven lamp stands
keys of seth

overcoming
second death

when did we fall in love with religion
instead of just loving God

the world has forsaken its one true love
and all the peoples of the earth shall mourn

until knowledge of self is as common as rain
or the pulsing of blood in the vibrating vein

i am a weary wormhole traveler
one who has endured to peer thru the veil of inner-stellar dust

i am but a speck on the cosmic mirror of dew reflection
the voice of he that crieth in the wilderness

the darkness is profound, but it is peace

SUPERNOVA

This book is dedicated to Clarity Dawn.
You taught me how to reach the younger
generation, and for that I am forever
in your debt.

A Brief History of Time
(a.k.a. you draw the tree)

Sleep is the cousin of Death
Life's little brother

two separate fathers
one distant mother

Time fathers Death and he cradles him hard
Life is the first born son of Sun-Ra

with Light as his twin they sought Peace through the land
and old mother Earth just kept dancing her dance

but one day,
as the story goes...

Sleep made a pact with old father Time
his pop cultured Mass Hypnosis lulled the blind

sharing the spoils of uncle War's greed
distracting the people, consuming Earth's seed

(tree)

now, Light was a playa
he ran the streets

Faith wuz his...
fairy godmother

and Life ain't really related to Sleep,
but he know he gotta find that ... m-f'er

Time and Sun-Ra had a father named God
seer, seeing and seen

Vision was down here mackin on Earth
that's why we got crazy dreams

so its Light and its Vision, and they searching for Peace
and Life is leading the pack

but you wouldn't notice, if you saw them creep
cause he always keep to the back

(tree)

suddenly Vision stops dead in his tracks
and he turns to Light and he says

i got it, naw really i got it
whachu do is you tell Faith to come with us

u tell Faith to bring her home girl Clarity
and come with us to talk to Death

he always was tryin to get next to Faith
and just cause i just think Clarity is fly

we bring them with us to holler at spooky young Death
and he gotta talk to his pops for us

he gotta talk to his crazy old pops for us all
and he gotta get him to stop this Madness

somebody please
stop the madness

Antichrist

starvation
profanity
outsourcing
extinct species
caste systems
global warming
cold war
reaping, sowing
hunger striking
profiling
unilateral sweat shop sightings
tsunamis
pollination
wild fires
deforestation
carbon output
co-payments
disintegrating glaciers
antartica
sheep cloning
gerrymandered, senate vote zoning
wire tapping
oil lovers
katrina
twelve year old mothers
gun runners
capital punishers
and the so-called war on terror
demagoguery
tax evasion
nuclear proliferation
brazillian kidnapped tenants
twelve million undocumented
green house effect
exxon lords
black on brown cali prison wars
west nile
ariel sharon
columbine
darfur
christian science
sean hannity
acquitted temporary insanity
slave mentality
indonesia
permafrost

shiite militias
chosen people
bar code implants
artificial intelligence
black hawks
dictators
9-11
governor terminator
afganistan
bomb prodigies
priest hood teenage sodomy
killer heat waves
opus dei
mass eugenics
guantanamo bay
the intifada, newly enlisted
a massacre by lebanese christians
retaliation
soul is the price
recipe book
anti-Christ

The Mic is the Evolution of the Mind

the mic is the evolution of the mind
the evolution is the mind of the rapper
the rapper is the mic of hip hop
hip hop is the mic of the evolution

all are intertwined

the mic, the mind, the rapper

hip hop, the evolution, you

we are one

Sestina in Black
a.k.a. Rainmaker #3

flames of old
resurrect anew
no rain for days, but there was the blackness
and it was beautiful
clouds. heavy stench of humidity and soot
ashen air choking, no space in my lungs
and that moment
that moment in time when the frozen moonlight
never ceases to break thru the top layered clouds
separating earth and space
and it seems like the fires may never cease
nothing but endless earth to burn consume and waste
(all those ideas, passions, moments) burn   b-u-r-n!
until the first rain drop: cool blue moist soothing icy liquid
pool of blackwashed puddle muddied and serene
and that moment
that moment when the first crack of lightning whips to the earth
shattering the black night, the still silence, the nothing
empty space, *get your buckets ready*
culture, a million and one stars all churning, all burning
cool – moist – smooth smoke expands
emanating trails thru the sky, endless eternity
the moon, the axis center of all space pulling on earth and blue water
the moon, its tears form rain
moon's reflection in pools of rain water
like an eye in the black space
cuts thru chilly midnight sky
moon's beats provide pulses of the universe
cycle of earth, replaces the sun in the sky
rhyming on the corner in the moonlight
moon seeps thru cracks of time
moon's love affair affair with the stars upsets the earth
course she always thought she was the center of the universe
and there was a time when there was nothing but beat
space and blackness was king
then earth was born, she brought sky – that eternal blue
timeless as its form
giver of life supporting rain

i'm gonna be a star
i'm gonna give my mentals enuff space to breathe in
only then will these fires be harnessed and churned into star form
otherwise it just burns

black people
magic people
spirit people
natural beat like mambo kings and blue note
the last guardians of rhyme
thudding of rain pitter patter on rooftops
clanking, blowing in chimneys, in sheets of downpour
monsoon of the messiah
rain on me
rain down on me

Don't Talk to Me About Love

don't talk to me about love in the beginning

you wait until things get rough

when the passion is gone
and the dream is deferred

only then can you talk to me
about love

one to one
like a true man

don't talk to me about love when its all wine and roses

chocolates and sweet nothings to get me through the night.

when its all stolen glances and foot massages
candle lit dinners and sandra bullock movies
massage oils and incense and coltrane and headboards

and don't get me wrong, i dig that stuff too
but that ain't the time to talk about love

you wait just a little while longer
wait until things get rough

talk to me about love when i'm out of luck
and you're out of work
and the rent's due
and the bills are late

talk to me about love when you're too proud to stand in line for a check
or i'm late for a job interview and the bus don't show

talk to me about love when the lights are cut off
when we've pawned your gold watch and my silver trumpet
when the neighbors are talking and the church members gossiping
and at candle lit dinners we toast bologna sandwiches

with no mustard

then you can talk to me about love

talk to me about love when our plans have died
when you're too busy to start up that business
and i'm too tired to go back to college

when the heat's cut off again and there's a leak in the roof,
and the health insurance won't cover a damn thing

talk to me about love when your parents hate me

when your pastor won't counsel us
because i'm southern baptist
and you're devout methodist

when my uncle is drunk at our family reunion
and the kids act a fool and the in laws keep arguing
and the bbq's burnt cause I never did like your mama's cookin no way,

that would be a good time to start talking to me about love

don't talk to me about love in the beginning
cause baby, that's just too easy
you wait just a little bit longer
to talk to me about love

when you can't stand my voice
and i can't stand your smell
when your teeth have gone yellow
and my love handle's sag

talk to me about love when the car payment's due
and the price of diapers has gone up again.
when the overcrowded school is just not good enough
for our attention deficit daughter,
or our son that's considering gang protection

talk to me about love when we're out marching for freedom
and our cell phone taps are clicking in the back ground

when our weekly trips to the open mic spot just don't cut it no more

talk to me about love when they come for me in the night

when one of us is on the run
and being hunted down for covert tactics
against a suppressive central power
that used to be a democracy
and now is just demon crazy

the kind of love that whispers through steel bars
and cries through plexi glass
cause your voice just don't sound right
on these tattered prison phones

the kind of love that waited for mandela
that waited for malcolm
and that waits for mumia even now as we speak

don't talk to me about love in the beginning

that's the easy part

you wait until things
get good and rough.

and then,
and only then
can you talk to me
about love

Pluto Ain't A Planet No Mo

i saw on the news, just the other day
pluto ain't a planet no mo
they cut inta "meet the press" just to say
that pluto ain't a planet no mo
the senate politico are scared and runnin away
i can't get news bout the troubles of my day
i'm more interested in what wall street got to say
but pluto ain't a planet no mo

said sumpin bout "fraction of an orbit is what we've learned"
so pluto ain't a planet no mo
3/5's of our populace can't live on what they earn
but pluto ain't a planet no mo
our ecosystem's a dangerous burn
my high school homie is startin a third term
the wheels of judgement day are starting to turn
but pluto ain't a planet no mo

maybe i'll write a letter to the station bout this blunder
pluto ain't a planet no mo
i liked my little 9th celestial wonder
pluto ain't a planet no mo?
we can't get a system to help crack mothers
might as well be worshipping the roman god of thunder
forget the solar system, our hoods are torn asunder
but pluto ain't a planet no mo

we turning youths into zombies, its called hypnotiz
but pluto ain't a planet no mo
i'd rather see another docu-drama on queen liz
than pluto ain't a planet no mo
we got rappers glorifying a life of madness
schools and prisons run by the very same biz
somebody tell the cops to stop beatin our kids
but pluto ain't a planet no mo

just a flashy example of where ignorance dwells
pluto ain't a planet no mo
the 6 o'clock news is worse than junk mail
and pluto ain't a planet no mo
those 5 cuban nationals still locked in they cell
they trickin' folks to believing that there ain't no hell
guess they all got no better lies to tell
than that pluto ain't a planet no mo

Poem for East and West Indian Inter-racial Dating

How can she love me if she does not understand me
Libertine lady of passion without peace
A genius enshrouded in paragon of wifey
Yet unwilling to tread the blackness of my sea
How can you love me if you do not understand me
O' copper toned Sheba of pralines and cream
You send me your love but it does not surround me
To you my struggles are a mere militant dream
You can not love me if you do not understand me
But I love you no less for your sheath
And I don't blame the play that your cast list is sounding
Nor the paleness in the way that you think

Fly Bicameral

the money controls the brain
the brain controls the man

motion to bomb a plan
Economic Hitman

the one who wears the pants
makes deals on foreign lands

they rape below the sand
drop guns in the frying pan

we add fuel to the fire
with aid to corporate buyers

funneled into the states
electronically cross the wires

been keepin' the methods veiled
with their f.b.i. bribers

and make the stories sell
by worshiping media liars

uproot the *seeds of peace*
with global hegemony

they feed us m.t.v.
while the oil feeds the beast

support the local elite
puppets on royal seats

a trillion dollar feat
for the corporatocracy

suppress the prophecy
supply demand for cheese

uphold the plan for ease
think fast like damocles

the scheme is to distract
and to distort spiritual leading

you need to be more worried
about your bicameral dreaming

upheave the need for heathens
and atheistic reasoning

like fish food for the needing
the lamb of ceasar bleeding

a loan shark to send out bets
that we cant pay

uphold the faith and slay
its death by foreign aid

make haste before the bomb hits
the clam without the walrus

but who's the real carpenter
sharpening swords of promise

they seek gold in the valley
not mastering the fall

there's more to time passing
than you consciously recall

the right brain battling logic
to feed the call

it ain't insane
the umbilical cord to god

fight for the mortal laws
original man is all

a cro magnum brawl
without the brain's applause

a call to reach the canopy
shifting how the planet moves

music be the hope
for kids to learn kinetic moves

flows be the bridge
only the sky can limit you

mind state damage you
fly bicameral

Conversations With Afternoon Rain

and so it begins, again,
the cycle of centrifugal motion.

inwardly scouring my spirit's ocean
seeking a cure for world pain

exhausted debating
and each party cowering

i seek out the wisdom
of the rain

they say rain falls in sheets,
i say it is more like a blanket

crowded pitter patters of nourishment and life
yet filled with the shroud of human contamination:

smog, petrol,
and acid filled strife.

burning the harvest of great western plains
choking the life from man's best plans laid

yet no news
of al gore for president

i do not blame him.
really

the age of gold reason has long since departed,
they now label treason what once was called martyr
and many a wise and mellifluous candidate
sullied from hype media 6 o'clock lore

and while I have pondered the purpose of adding
a sacrificed lamb to the lost chamber clapping
to senate and house representatives napping
when called to the voting upon chamber floors

the rain said to listen, to listen once more

'to what' i entreated, 'tis leadership needed
and honor and courage, integrity's door
to open with passion while righteousness' rations
could feed twice the masses of our border's shores

the rain said to listen, to listen once more
only of this and of nothing more

of what to take notice, a generation hopeless
a glorified era of drugs, sex and booze
pop culture is fiendish, we should be world leaders
our youth spend their young lives all blazed and confused

we've got pushers and peddlers and pedophiliac predators
pedagogic lecturers sexing their students
rehab abusers and hypocritical blessers
famous cross dressers, the stars just keep cruising

we idolize deviance, glorify meaningless
jingles and one hit wonder catchy tunes
we commercialize lunacy, payoff buffoonery
and fill every young dream with new nike shoes

any new pleasure, the poison to choose
to keep us distracted from the real world news

an answer, i'm wishing, or one simple mission:
to rise from this valley of national glue
the serpent is hissing, the pentagon's kissing
our deep set addiction to these fossil fuels

we're abetting and aiding a crusade generation
that's bent on creating imperial tours.
a slave to the lie of decreasing F5's,
the schemes and jet streams we're convinced to ignore

tis equal to blood soaked on il goree's door

the rain said to listen, to listen once more
only of this, and of nothing more

its freedom on trial with health care denial
and poor schools, no pensions, and immigrant cots
its red tape and therapy for 20 year old veterans,
the plunder, the gunpowder, treason and plot

we're soaked to our cuticles, lies cruel and unusual
those rights once inalienable are now filled with lead
our classmates are sleepless with nights in falluja
and tortured back home like guantanamo bed

they'll suck out our hopes till the last drop is dead

ah hem

at last the rain decided to speak
and this is what she finally said

had it pleased heaven to dry me with depletion,
had they rained all types of terrors and consolations upon my shores,
steeped me into fluro-carbons to the very brink,
given to captivity me and my utmost hope;
I should have found in some place of my nimbus
a taste for freedom. but alas,
to make me the fixed figure for the age of technology
to point its soulless and webbed finger at.
yet, could I bear that too
well, most well
but there. where i have garnered up my roots,
where either i must give or bear no fruit
the promise from the which my seedling runs
must be burnt up or discarded hence
or, keep it as a sketch book for young lives to joke at on saturday night
turn thy shackles there;
freedom, thou thrice abused operation.
'tis sacrilege for the price of black ore

only this, and nothing more

Khonsu and Dawn

The first memory that comes to mind when I think about New York is the subway, and I couldn't talk about Black if I didn't talk about the city.

The 6 train was a deceptive clean. It was about as sanitary as anything in the city could hope to be, yet somehow dingy in its hygienic upkeep, especially thru the mud and the sweat of late summer rain. Its so freakin' humid out here. The rain barely washes away the sweat and the grime and the funk of the city. I'll never forget the bright fluorescent glow as you step into the car, such a contrast from the dingy dull buzz of the rest of the subway station. Neon red lights that flash the departing stop, and the double ding of some invisible bell proudly proclaiming that the "doors are about to close."

Naw, I don't think I'll ever forget that monotone automated electronic voice of indifference that somehow manages to sound amiable in the shuffle and the scurry of the train. Bing-bong. 77th street and a mink scarfed lady with her French poodle dripping wet. She plunges into the car and barely grabs hold of the double doors as they slide into place. I don't even know how Su managed to scoop that poodle in before the leash caught hold as the train scooted away. But he always was quick with things like that. Reflex motions, I guess. "Had a little trouble with the door, huh?. . . You alright lady?"

That's my brother, Su. His real name is Khonsu. He was named after the Egyptian God of the moon. Su is just what he goes by. Figured it'd be easier. People always wanna know what kinda hippie parents you got, and that leads to a whole string of embarrassing questions.

"Come on Dawn; let's let this lady have our seat." We get up, and move to the corner of the car. I like the subway. It reminds me of the rock of the ocean when you go limp and just let your body drift. I wish I dug my new school as much as I liked the train. P.S. 109 was overcrowded, understaffed and as fiercely bi-lingual as any place I'd ever seen. But some of the kids were cool.

Out of all the New Yorkers I've met, I think I like Joi the best. She's from the Far East; studies modern dance at some movement studio in The Village. I don't understand why someone would want to move to a humongous city just to hang out in a village.

Me and Khonsu grew up in Venice.

We were used to the lapping rock of the sunny pacific—an almost mantra-esque chanting of the great blue beyond—playing soundtrack for the wacky hustler parade of artists, bums and dharma bums that make up the cali boardwalk. I guess who I miss most is Simplicity. She used to stroll the sidewalks of southern Cali like no one I'd ever seen. I once heard she walked from the Chinese theatre all the way to the Ferris Wheel, in one afternoon. Not that it's possible but, you can guess how avidly the legend of Simplicity grew.

The trip out here was a trip in itself. Venice to Harlem in a greyhound. After awhile the desolate rest stops blend together, a head rattlingly bumpy carpet ride through a vast nebulous of sand and funky bathrooms, one cactus to the next. San Bernadino to Flagstaff. Flagstaff to Albuquerque, a long cold night, and you wake up in El Paso. Then it's on to Fort. Worth and Oklahoma City, up to Fayetteville and Louisville. We stopped for half and day or so and made the slow, grinding drive into the east coast: Baltimore, (some little town in Penn,) Philly, Trenton, Newark and finally, the Big Apple itself. All in all not a bad week.

I try to live in the city, and not be of the city, and I write letters home to Simplicity.

So really the only person I hang with a lot down here is Faith. She's the realest.

I think Su's friend Juan Carlos has a thing for her. She don't really speak much Spanish, but just the fact that she's learning with him I think was really the turn on. I don't know why she seems so into Vision. I don't know, he just rubs me the wrong way, mastermind meditating money wheels, constantly turning and spinning out his next devious move. Yeah, he'll take over something alright, but I wonder what.

And really, that's who got Khonsu all mixed up with Black Vengeance. But they didn't call him that till later on.

"C'mon Most Royal Dawn, you gotta show me your poem thing. How else am I supposed to put my skills on Joi?"

"If you had skills you wouldn't need me to help you do anything."

Its interesting how we can repeat and illusion so many times until we ourselves mistake it for reality. So anyways, I'm showing Vision this essay-type poem thing I wrote about Joi, really just cause he kept hounding me about it. We were all out at Mart 125, just messin with the rastas and lookin at jeans. They changed The Mart after 9/11 is what Vision told me. Had to keep it fenced in this parking lot. Supposedly it used to be a whole experience to walk through Harlem and browse the sidewalk bodegas, white folks looking for black soap and every now and then a teenager sittin right on the sidewalk getting his hair twisted up in locks for the first time. But I didn't get to see any of that. What I saw was more like, some kinda vendor's refugee camp. They had everybody all packed in these little rows, the smell of incense, oils and shea butter barely overcrowding the blare of dancehall music and rap. I dunno, kinda felt a prison yard to me. It was like … well, I'm tryin to keep it all on the positive in this journal. My last diary got kinda crazy. I guess you could say my journal entries fight off depression sometimes, all in the name of good therapy of course. It didn't even make sense until I sent all my diary letters to Simplicity. She always knew what to say. Anyways, this is the joint I wrote about Joi:

Joi is a secret. You have to work to find it, and work to keep it.
the powers that be wanna steal it, that they too may one day
know its strength and silent validity.
the dark side may have the power of rage,
but we have the power of joy.
what is possessing the secret of joy?
to be firm and unquestioningly resolute in the love that feeds it.
to be secure and completely satisfied in the ease that binds it to you.
and to rest easy in the comfort that it brings.
possessing joy is at all times a source to attack
for it is the one thing that can not be stolen away.
they must attack it from within.
they must seek to infiltrate through fears and delusions
and misunderstandings made complicated.
joy and clarity go hand in hand.
you can not have the one without the other.
imagine how much joy we would truly find
in the most mundane of every day life
if we clearly understood the magnitude of the creator's master plan.

the peace and the happiness and the life and the light that is in store
for every living creature and which already resides in them.
how we would rejoice at the mere sight of a smile
or a sparkle, a stolen moment of truth between two passers by.
joy is the secret that lies hidden among us
and it is the power that lies within.
seek it
and it will find you

That's what I wrote about Joi. And sometimes its like, wow, ya know? You'll go back to some old journal entry you haven't read in weeks and think, there's no way I wrote that. But I did.

Juan Carlos has this friend named Spiritual. He's mad intense, but somehow calm and gentle at the same time. Caribbean cat, I think he's from Barbados or Grenada, something like that. I never met his brother, but I heard he has a twin named Mysticism.

I think the term is, they fought like the dickens? Anyways, it was me and Su, and we were at the park right off of FDR Drive, watchin the Puerto Ricans play baseball. They're out there every Saturday; it's the highlight of my week. And so I'm going for the El Barrio team cause, that's my hood ya know? But the guys from the Bronx keep staring us up and down, cause I guess we're wearing the wrong colors or whatever. The Barrio Ballers verses the Bronx Brawlers. Yeah, try sayin that a buncha times fast. And so these Bronx kids start messing with me and Su and, I mean, now I know why he works so hard to be so cool. It is hard work. People mess with you. But he told me a long time ago, he said "Dawn, I work hard to not have a temper, because that's never proper etiquette. That would lower us. We are kings and queens, and royalty should never lower themselves." That's what he said.

But yeah, I don't know what would've happened to us if Black hadn't shown up.

I can't say that I like him, he's sort of the resident D-Bo for the neighborhood; but I gotta admit he bailed us out that day.

Really, he bailed me out that day.

See, I was kinda in to talking mess cause we were the new kids on the block and all- really, no pun intended – and I guess some guys that were there to see the Bronx team didn't like some… things that I was saying, some personal things, that perhaps shouldn't be said, in a park … about someone's mother or whatever. And so next thing I know, I'm surrounded by the concessions stands and all— grown man behind the counter can sell me a hot dog but can't say a word to some young punks— and out of all the guys its some short, scrubby looking, some 5 foot nothin' guy that actually grabs my jacket collar. Can you believe he even had a cross around his neck, matching the faded gold on his front tooth.

And in the middle of all this, who shows up? Black.

"Y'all Ricans is 'bout to bite off more than y'all can chew. Leave the little sister alone."

He had a voice like cold thunder, like when the weather shifts all of a sudden and the sky goes from blue to dark grey. It reminded me of this guy that Su used to play on cassette tapes; old speeches from Paul Robeson. I never knew you could feel comfort and fear at the very same time. But there it was in 6 foot denim. There's only one other person I know who's voice can ring like thunder, but his cracks with lightning at the very same time. Thank goodness I never saw Juan Carlos get mad until way, way later.

As a matter of fact, that's who appeared out of nowhere to calm the whole situation. See, I guess the Nuyoricans— as these Bronx kids liked to call themselves— weren't used to being confronted. I swear, every bird in the park stopped chirping as Black and his crew squared off with the flock; a buncha high yellow cowards if you ask me. It was like one of those old movies with the slow music and the white guy in a poncho. Everything stopped. We all just stood there eyeing each other in the stiff silence and the heat and the swelling humidity of the inner city day.

Khonsu is holding a handful of rocks. The kids from the Bronx got beer bottles and what looked like an ice pick. I could smell the breath from that 5 foot nothin' kid as he finally let go of my windbreaker. It smelled like cheap beer and Arros con pollo. Yuck. And Black is pullin something from his back pocket, but I never had time to see.

"Peace be upon you. All of you." (I'll give you one guess who it was.) He spoke with the conviction of a criminal lawyer, and the softness of a brand new father. His large brown eyes swelled with the passion of a revolutionary, and yet somehow his gaze was as clear as a cloudless sky.

"Why do you look at the speck of dust in your brother's eye and pay no attention to the dirt in your own? How can you say to your brother 'brother, let me take the dust out of your eye,' when you yourself fail to see the grime in your own? You hypocrites, first wipe the soot from your own eyes, then you will see clearly to remove the speck from your brothers'. If you are good only to those who are good to you, what credit is that to you? Even the wicked love those who are good to them. And if you love only those who repay you, what good is that to you? Even Giuliani loves the one who lines his pockets. But love your enemies, do good to them, and lend to them without expecting to get anything back. No good tree bears bad fruit, nor does a bad tree bear good fruit. Each tree is recognized by its own. People do not pick mangos from thorn bushes, nor do they pull grapes from briars. The good man brings good things out of the good stored up in his heart. And the evil man brings evil things out of the evil stored in his. I tell you, love your enemies, as you would love yourself. Then your reward will be great, and you will be sons of the Most High. Be merciful, just as your Father is merciful."

And then the cops showed up.

Too many minorities in one park at one time.

Long story short, the nuyoricans scatter, Su is in cuffs, Black gets slammed on a police car, and Juan Carlos is the one that actually takes a nightstick to the head. I always told him he should've pressed charges, but he didn't. And that was it. We all went home. But I'll never forget that day. Of course the story ballooned over time, there were fifty Puerto Ricans and Black took a stun gun to the face by the time Vision was through with it. And ever since then all of Harlem seemed to know my name. We were El Barrio royalty as far as they were concerned, and to tell ya the truth it was kinda cool. I still get spooked out if I have to walk past the park at night. But I'll always remember the day I went from somebody's little sister, to the Most Royal Dawn.

A Patch Of Blue

A new play
By Julian Nyles Thomas

Based on the true story of Charles Bishop

This play was first produced at Northwestern University as part of a festival of ten minute plays. 100 Minutes of Theatre was put on by a group of theatre majors known simply as The Ensemble. In an attempt to acclimate the student campus to themes and issues that we felt were pertinent to the times we conducted a group project to produce a series of ten plays that we felt encapsulated the era. This is one of those plays.

A pause: a theatrical tool used to emphasize a heavy moment. Shorter than
A beat: a theatrical tool used to emphasize a heavy moment. Shorter than
A silence: a theatrical tool…

Scene 1. No Rule Against It

Teenager, boy or girl, dressed in baggy clothes. Very excited.

Alright so what I saw was…
well first there was the sound of the helicopter comin round the building over there
And it was loud man,
I mean like loud.
And all these sun tanned Tampa residents on the street are pointin and shoutin
"get down, get down,"
eyes all big and all, ya know?
Felt like I was in one of those old school war movies,
like it's the Viet-Cong or something, you know what I'm saying?

People is droppin their shopping bags and runnin behind cars,
behind those blue post office slots,
behind anything,
just to get out of the way and close their eyes like that's gonna make it all go away.
(pause)
But it didn't.
(pause)
And so finally I see this little airplane makin a sharp turn,
Look like something one of the wright brother's flew in,
old school propelors and everything
And he's makin this leisurely turn round the downtown buildings.
Now I'm just tryin to walk the rest of my 5 blocks home so's
I can get some rest 'fore evening service.
I mean its Sunday man, what's with all this commotion?
Don't y'all know it's the day of rest?
But all of a sudden its like…
Well hell man, I could tell that the plane was getting ready to run into the bank building.
A-a-a-nd it looked like the guy in the helicopter was trying to tell him something,
But he didn't listen,
Wasn't even lookin,
And then…oh my god man,
This plane is about to hit the building.
Somebody do something, call the cops or somethin.
I'm standin there yelling for a cell phone or, or anything
And everybody's just frozen solid.
Like, you coulda heard a pin drop.
(beat)
And then boom!
He flew right into that bank building.
Didn't even slow down or nothin man, it was like…
I mean it was crazy man.
And then, and then,

It was just the white tail of the plane man,
(beat)
Stickin halfway out the grey concrete slab of building,
(pause)
Against a sky so clear
so blue,
you woulda thought it was a painting or something.
It was so still just lyin up there
halfway in and halfway out.
And then the cops get there with their yellow police tape,
Holding everybody back, telling me to go home.
(silence)
So I left,
Went home to catch the 6 o'clock news.
(beat)
And would you believe what they said?
(beat)
It was a 15 year old kid in the plane man,
By himself!
Are you freakin freakin kidding me?
I didn't even know you could take flying lessons that young.
And they leave him in the plane
alone,
with the keys?
Where was his flight instructor?
Where was his parents?
And they talking about,
"no regulations were violated in leaving him alone for the preflight check."
What kinda fool leaves a kid in the pilot's seat of a plane by himself?
And then the news lady is interviewing this little boy who went
To school with him, and he's all saying how the boy would
sit in the back of the bus everyday with dark sunglasses
never spoke to nobody.
C'mon man,
that's the kind of kid you leave in a plane by himself?
(Beat)
You gotta be kidding me.
(silence)
But the flight instructor gets off scot free just because there was
no rule against it.
I mean that's crazy man .
A 15 year old kid just die,
but he's not to blame
And that's it man, over and done,
There was just no rule against it.

Scene 2: Too Late

Flight instructor Carl Mason.
Male, age 30-40, wearing a short brown leather jacket.

15 year old Charles Bishop.
Wanted me to call him Charley.
He said that was what his friends called him
and that he wanted for us to be friends.
(silence)
He had been coming to ClearWater flight school for months,
It was a fluke, we don't just hand out keys to anybody.
I…thought he was doing a routine pre-flight check.
I never thought that
(pause)
It is not uncommon for an instructor to let a student do a preflight check alone,
We had done many together before.
A student can not get a pilot's license until age 17,
A student can not train alone until age 16.
He had been showing up for weeks, washing planes just to rack up airtime minutes.
he was so eager to learn.
He
(pause)
They said they found a letter, a suicide note,
Saying that he crashed the plane in support of Bin Laden and the Al Quaida.
(beat)
I only left him for a minute.
I heard the engine starting up but by the time I got back to the runway it was too late.
We sent out a coast guard copter from Tampa
and called ahead to the Clearwater International Airport.
Thank god we did.
He almost collided with a southwest airline boeing 747.
All those people, and
(beat)
and when he flew over airspace at the MacDill base
they scrambled for E15 fighters from the FAA
to patrol the area, not to intercept the plane.
But they were too late anyway.
He never even lost control of the air craft.
The plane never made any sudden moves or anything,
A smooth 100 mph right until
(beat)
And I radioed to him and we all signaled for him to just land.
I told him it would be okay,

that I wouldn't even tell his grandmother about the mix up,
if he would JUST
(beat)
AGREE
(beat)
to LAND.
But we were all too late.
(silence)
and now this note about the Al Quaida.
The most alarming thing was that he left an intelligent letter,
a manifesto, shouting his beliefs to the world.
This is not a case of them using our own weapons against us,
this is our youth, our number one resource as a nation.
And for him to act on such a, passionate belief,
I, well that's what keeps me up at night.
(beat)
My flight school was used as a tool, this young life...
and every night I think about that one minute I left him in the plane,
one minute was all it took to get that plane into the air
and in that one minute he could've been saved.
(beat)
He even managed to take out ten feet in the Bank of America Plaza,
But that was just a lot of window space.
He wasn't much of a threat.
Its like driving a car into a tree.
Who's gonna get hurt?
The people in the car.
(silence)
It might mean better enforcement of the laws,
It might mean new legislation,
What that boy needed was someone to reach out to.
And we were just too late.
(pause)
all of us,
we were all just too late.

Scene 3: He Was Such A Nice Boy

An attractive young teacher, female, sitting on a teacher's desk.

You know,
In the newspapers, on TV,
All they talk about is how lonely Charley was,
How he didn't have any friends.
But he was such a nice boy.
Every morning I would show up kind of nervous-
Its my first year teaching and all-
And every morning I could look to the back row
And get just the warmest smile from this little curly haired boy.
(Beat)
He was a typical gangly 15 year old with an acne problem
And a passion for flying.
(pause)
He gave me more encouragement than he could ever know.
And all the other freshmen at East Lake High would try to get over on me,
They'd play little pranks or switch around the time schedule,
Anything to take advantage of the new teacher.
But Charley…he would just sit in the back and stare out the window.
I'm a day dreamer myself and I think its healthy, especially for young people,
To let their minds stretch out sometimes.
But Charley would always speak up whenever I called on him.
I remember back in September we all had discussions on the New York incident.
And he was saddened by the loss of life.
He wanted to join the air force.
I mean, he was a flag bearer and everything.
Bright, disciplined, well liked…he may not have been the most popular of students
But you know what, he always had a smile on his face.
(Beat)
He was always pleasant and respectful,
We had absolutely no idea that this might occur.
(Silence)
You know, kids give signs when they need help,
Its our job to see them.
When something like this approaches you usually see a behavior change,
They might loose weight
Or grades will suddenly drop.
Some kids become isolated and argumentative.
They start giving away things dear to them.
But anger held inside and allowed to bubble,

That's the major culprit.

This kind of thing doesn't just happen out of the blue.

(Beat)

We HAVE to become better listeners.

More skillful at spotting the clues.

Let them know that we care enough to notice their loneliness and their anger.

Sure, this particular incident may have been avoided if the flight instructor

Went out with the student while he was performing his…preflight-whatever…

But if you block one door

And if you have a person dedicated to committing suicide,

They will find another door.

Or they'll make a window.

(pause)

And you know what, he was one of the only two students

That gave me a card and a gift before Christmas break.

It was a special mug that he said was just perfect for hot chocolate.

Just perfect

Scene 4: BLOODBROTHERS

Emerson Favreau. Boy, 15, dressed in bright clothes and sneakers.

Charley was my friend.
We would chat for hours at night after our parents thought we were asleep.
I mean I thought it was weird that his IM name was "hopeless"
But I never teased him or nothing,
I just thought he was different,
But that's what I liked about charley,
He was.
Different, I mean.
(beat)
I remember reading Romeo and Juliet in class before winter break,
Everyone was crying by the end.
Even most of the guys.
But Charley, it didn't even phaze him.
I mean, I guess he looked kinda sad but he didn't shed a tear or anything.
He would just stare out of the window and I figured he was
Day dreaming about flying or something and I knew how much he loved it
sailing thru the clouds, high enough to touch the sun.
(pause)
He didn't even say goodbye.
(pause)
And on the news, in the papers
They just kept repeating "its not terrorism, its not terrorism"
Then what the hell was it?
And no one at school would even talk about it.
Everybody knew him,
I mean,
I just think about all the people he could've said goodbye to,
That he could've hung out with before…
And what was the last thing I said to him?
Typed to him on the computer.
I don't even think I ever told him how good a friend he was to me.
(beat)
How can somebody choose to die?
I just don't get it.
I don't think he supported Bin Laden at all.
I think he wrote that in the note just to get attention.
He always wanted to leave his mark on the world
he didn't wanna hurt anybody.
(Beat)

And he even told me to watch the news that night,
He said to be sure I didn't miss it.
That no matter what we would always be
Blood brothers.
Well he might not have wanted to hurt anybody
But he sure hurt me,
(Pause)
He didn't even say goodbye.
(Pause)
He didn't even mention his family in the note or nothin.
It was like he just up and decided one day that it wasn't worth it anymore.
Bin Laden didn't have anything to do with that.
Charlie didn't deserve all this, he just felt like he had no other choice.
People are gonna remember him as this crazy kid who went nuts one day.
But charley wasn't like that.
Deep down I think he was just misunderstood.
But I guess we all are.
I know I am.

Scene5: NOBODY CARES

Charlie's Grandmother.
An old woman, a rocking chair, and a cane.
She is holding a newspaper in her hands.

Such a smart boy.
Such a clever boy.
He always wanted to fly.
I barely walked thru the door
From dropping Charley off at flight school
And his mother is on the phone.
(pause)
She looked so scared.
(silence)
And right away I knew,
I knew it was charley.
And the whole time I was telling his mother,
Something is wrong, he don't need to spend so much time
Upstairs in his room.
He come home from school and that's all he do,
Just sit in front that computer.
He don't talk to us,
He don't eat nothing.
(beat)
I thought it was, some girl at school,
Maybe he was upset because his acne medication not working.
Doctors put him on…Accutane.
They say that's what made him depressed.
But Charley wasn't depressed.
He loved his flying lessons.
It was just good to see him finally interested in something.
I drove him to his lesson that day.
We were celebrating cause he just got straight A's on his grade card
And all he talked about was wantin to fly.
I had to chase the reporters away with this very cane.
They show up that same night to talk to his mother.
What kind of decency IS that?
He was so happy during the ride out there.
Just beaming in his seat and staring out the window.
And all of a sudden he turn to me and say
"grandma, if something happens to me,
don't let any of my enemies come to my funeral."

I say what kind of enemies a 15 year old boy have?
He just smile and look out the window.
(beat)
I don't blame the flight school, and I don't blame his teachers,
WE should have seen something.
We should have known.
(pause)
and now it is too late.
(beat)
how could this not be on the front page of the New York Times?
The teenage version of the world trade center they call it,
But that not good enough to be front page news, huh?
And what is President Bush doing about this?
How many people have to die before it becomes front page news?
Nobody cares until is their son or their daughter in the plane.
(pause)
Charley was a good boy.
(pause)
And he never harm nobody.
(silence)
I sit in this house
And I can almost hear him up there,
Typin' away upstairs.
But that's all over now.
And somehow, somehow we find the strength
And the courage to go on.
I've lived to see this country thru many wars.
But this one's different.
This time they attack us in our own homes,
Our own children.
(pause)
This does not end with Charley, this is only the beginning.
One day, maybe we look back and be proud of Charley for what he did.
Maybe he knew something we don't.
But right now, I grieve for this young life.
And I know one day, I will see his smiling face again.
So no goodbye's and no farewells.
But everytime I see that blue sky out my windowpane,
I know
Charley is watching.
And I know he has all the space to fly
That he will ever need.

BONUS SECTION:

MANTRAS, PRAYERS, NOTES, SONGS AND AFFIRMATIONS

Make It Funky

I pledge allegiance to the funk
The united funk of funkadelica
And to the republic for which it jams

with the united funk
we funk

I pledge allegiance . . .

Which came first, the funk or the cool?

The question is, can you be funky without first being cool?

I think not.
Funk is a physiological phenomenon where
individuality meets creativity and no, I think it would take
a cool person to find that funk in the first place.

So cool was first?

Well, in order for the cool to survive and be passed on
there had to be funky places where it could find a groove.

What is a funky place?

Well first off what is a funky person?

An individual.
Someone who feeds on being different
But not only that, they have to have their own style.
So if I painted my seabring black and white cow spots
and sported a cap like the mad hatter everywhere I went
does that count as my style?

Maybe. Well no,
it depends on why I'm wearing the cap,
and in this case I most definitely wouldn't be doing it
for any sort of right reason.

What signifies style is a level of coolness that transcends
public opinion.

So if I'm doing and wearing these things
just to be different, no, I don't think that counts.

But to get back to the heart of the matter, funk is what hits
you deep down. That spot inside your chest or a rhythm that
Makes you shake yo' groove thang.
Funk can not be disguised.
Its intrusive its loud and its free.
Funk is you, funk is me,
For many people its kinda scary.
There's some people that can't handle hot funky love making.
You know, you got that slow sensual smooth type of run my fingers
Thru your hair sexing.
And then there's the bootie slappin, legs on your shoulder, high
Pitched squeakin, candle wax drippin (for the voyeurs)
Deep down funky kinda sex.
But that's not everybody's thing
And I respect that

So what is funk?

Sly stone's sweat socks and james' brown greasy cloak.
Jimi's headband and badu's green eyes.
From stankonia to bitches brew its guitar picks and collard greens,
Hot sauce on chicken wings
Digable planets, true funkanauts, yet so before
Their time. dennis rodman, george clinton, bill clinton,
and hillary rodham . . .

it s colorful, its vibrant, but most of all its alive and free
funk is you, funk is me funk is us funk is we…

if the cool wuz the beginning
the funk is the hereafter

funk is brer rabbit and king louie slammin up earth on a
dr. dre beat. Funk is the rhythm of the stars, the everlasting
heartbeat. Funkalicious dancehall blisters the size of the
whelps that Foreman got from Ali, or warm chai tea
that goes down strong like Leon Phelps.

Yes,
the rhythm of the juke joint and the rhythm of the sea,
funk is you funk is me funk is us funk is we
the rhythm in you, and the life pulse in me,
funk is you funk is me funk is us funk is free
funk is you funk is me funk is us funk is we . . . .

A Brief History of Time Supplement

you see, Peace resides with Time

and that's why they out looking for Sleep

(you know, Life, Vision, Faith and the gang)

cause Sleep's the only one that really knows how to find Peace

Death, being Sleep's first cousin and all, is the only one
     on good terms with Sleep

(Sleep is too strong for his own good right now what with
     Mass Hypnosis running rampant,
      eating all the pop charts on Earth and all)

and so they figure,
if they can find Death they can find Sleep
if they can find Sleep they can find Peace
if they can find Peace than BlackLife
will be whole again

and Black Vengeance will be no more

somebody scream

An Excerpt From "Autumn Leaves"
(one of the next books coming soon)

she hates 'em both,
you know

the store bought status quo classical
and the underground hookup

studio religion
and free spirit mysticism
        she hates 'em both

God that is

            God is worship
                God is love
                    that is all

indulgence is a sign of weakness
and being sentimental is like checking into rehab
        let it go and move on

you've got to write it all down
so says charles wright

and so says i
you've got to write it down, julian

        love lost memories, sleepless nights, you've got
        to write it all down

        short breathed and heart thumping in the cold of
        the morning, misplaced affection from half fooled
        love dream, watery eyes from an ex's favorite song,
        you've got to write it all down

        zoned out longing from shadowy memory,
        nostalgic smile at teen vampire novel . . .

every true artist is hyper emotional. it is the sacred
feminine unlocked within. tumultuous and free,
impassioned and unhindered, your generation will
understand the pain. they feel it as you do
write it all down

if i can talk to God like she's my daddy
i can talk to my brother like he's my brother

and i can talk to Christ like he's my best homie

can u dig it?

Khonsu's Prayer

In the name of Jesus,
Lord, thank you for waking me up today
Thank you for keeping me safe while I slept
And thank you for Dawn
Thank you for Joy and thank you for Courage
And thank you for delivering us all from Evil
Lord, keep me on your path as I travel thru out my day
In Jesus, keep me in your walk and your light and your
Way. Continue to strip my bark until I am nothing
But solid wood. continue to strip me down until my desires
Are your desires, until my thoughts are your thoughts,
until my mind moves like yours
I ask these things in the name of your son, Jesus
Christ, and I thank you once again, for Deliverance.
--Ahmen

The road to Pure Being

1. So its five installments of nine dimensions:
(and that's the poetry shows I perform)

The Oriental Perspective
La Sacre feminie (The Sacred Feminine)
Australopithecus

Bicameralism
Negritude
Lifemind

Math/science/physics Numbers/stats . . .
The Theatre perspective
The Childlike perspective

(the first shall be last, the last shall be first)

2. And then you're installed in Joules
        (creative consciousness
        "this is why i'm hot"
        the methodology of awareness)

3. From there, we talk about Christ
                we talk about Muhommed
                we talk about the Dalai Llama
                        (metaphysics of peaceful revolution)

4. Pitfalls of the sacred path

5. Then you get your Christmind
What is christmind?

ChristMind

Christ body Christ body
Holy holy surely surely

Christ body Christ body

Christ

Christ mind lifemind represent the other side/ see me when I walk with the flame / so y'all ain't left behind / I gotta speak it but I ain't Jehova's witness / see them talk about

The future like they only ones that get it / but imma spill it cause I got it in my system / See my cup it runneth over like the fred price mission / the holy spirit got me wrapped up tight / and the blanket be the holy word / its holdin me right / yeah / if you ain't got it then you prob'ly not goin get it / and I only speak in riddles for the people that goin fear it / I fight the system till they crucify / but the truth is that I spit it cause I got the gab its / a way of livin stay afloat for the mission / and I order you to jump from the boat if you can swim it / I gotsta get it anyway that I can grab it / so the rest of y'all just dig on deeper flows and try to grasp it / the one objective is a state of pure livin / if you digging this then meet me on the road to damscus / I had to give up all the ignorant bliss / [I woke up one mourning ned flanders of this rap / ish /]

Joules T / the big cahuna / fly fishin for them demons / turning posers to tuna / yeah / gotta reclaim language / take the terms that they stole from us back / to the rhythm of spanglish / gotta study latin and the Aramaic pages / mix oriental with African slang its / true forms give us understanding / the way the Christ moved when you see it he demanding / a lot more from the people with heart / givin in to submission saw my rivers done part / started trippin on the holy greasy / woke up / found the celly / called up sister mary breezy / I said that I'm swimming in the rapture of wind / head swole from the power / just give me a pen / yeah / she said / slow down take a breath / stop and look at the yellow road you just left / then I said thru the nights they be givin me lead / the valley of the dead / I agree she said / but don't heed the fear / and don't give in / and when you see the shadows move just look for the footprints / I told her peace / told her bout baby's eyes / and learn to cook a meal cause leadership comin by / I said I got a recipe sure to make reign / team her up with clarity / sure to make change / yeah / that's right / a jesus freak / on the road I always tell the truth / even when its lies to you / we can't see but we goin make it to the finish line / its right there the goal line / right behind the scrimmage line /

Who am I / the truth and the life / on the road always goin right / a seeker for eternal light / spoke needle poems thru the humble camel's eye / voice in the wilderness I'm cryin at night / said the darkness will hide me / and the light become night / even the night's gonna shine / darkness its goin be my light / I got endurance forever / and a crown made of thorns / inherited the charge but I'm second born / the little brother in the fam / make heaven and earth sing / stood godfather for Malcolm and king /

took the flame to the booth / I got the shine for the west / try to give these ladies knowledge / why they givin me stress / got a girl for the future / ride a Mercedes / Imma call her leader ship cause her waters run deep / I know this girl named Rebecca / she got the courage to teach / the wife of Isaac got a mind for the Cherokee beat / Firefly be the illest / a soul sista for keeps / she inherited the charge / I call her esther peace / and elizabeth's holy / she got the fruit gonna bear / the dopest poet on the mic go by Jessica care / makeda she travel / she get to healin me up / that's my rainbow in the sky / she the queen of sheba / yeah / sarah the shy / she a fly actress Persian / in Oklahoma city gave the birth of a nation / rahab help me sneak fugitives of the world / ain't cha baby mama / she my geisha girl / yeah

Bicameral notes:

consciousness itself is what records
and stores our experiences
as they happen,

thereby it is said to form
the chief attribute of our definitive selves;

All of this is false.
That is the veil of consciousness

Consciousness does not pervade all mentality

what you can consciously recall
is but a thimbleful next to the ocean of your actual knowledge

bicameralism is a state of mind, its a conscious unlocking of the hyper sensitive
state, the creative crazy. and maintaining that funk in your every day

Ultimate bottom line quick analysis:

Consciousness is not something that is a slow, steady, predictable outcome of millions of years of physical evolutionary processes from amoeba to men, rather it is a fairly recent- last few millennia- emergent property of human culture. I.e.- while the Cro-Magnon tribes of 10,000 years ago, & even the early Middle Eastern cultures of 3 or 4,000 years ago, were filled with humans that were physiologically indistinguishable from Modern Man, they were- on a psychological level- fundamentally different. They were de facto zombies lacking a sense of the 'I'. Their brains functioned naturally on what we would today call a schizophrenic level- but they were not schizoid, this was their natural or (to use Cyber Age jargon) 'default' state of being. The brains of these people functioned bicamerally- that is their 2 hemispheres were at odds with each other. The Left was where the mortal man resided, going through tasks in a rote autonomic way- even if laughing or crying, while the Right was the demesne of the Gods.

Taking it back further, all the way indeed to the first organized off spring of Australopithecus Africanus (we're talking some 80,000 years ago at this point) their cultures contained a tribal figure who was set aside to assist in spiritual matters. When the ancient prophets had visions they were not crazy, it was this God-self (what might today be recognized as intuition) giving warnings or advice in the manner of voices &/or hallucinations. But, then society complexed to the point that more direct modes of thought predominated. The Egyptians, Olmecs, and even original Orientals, all black men by birth, heritage and skin tone, formed more distinct functions with their primitive mental aspects.

This bicamerality soon was remnant only in the disaffected & or mentally ill.

Julian Jaynes attempts to shed some light on the issue in his famous seventies psychology exploration:
"The Origin of Consciousness in the Breakdown of the Bicameral Mind"

look it up
look it up

Bicameralism

+ so, now there's a mary

- there's always been a bloody mary

+ a bloody mary and a bloody maria

- right. now there's an ave maria,

and there's a bloody bushdoctor …

+ well, what's a bloody bushdoctor?

- a bushdoctor is patron,

patron and pineapple juice

+ a bloody mary is vodka and tomato juice right?

- and a bunch of random stuff, yeah

+ so … a bloody bushdoctor is …

tomato juice and patron?

- no. tomato juice and tequila is a bloody maria

+ oh, that's right. so what's an ave maria?

- you don't wanna know

+ ok….

- a mary is just vodka and pineapple juice

+ and a rimshot of mango yes i know,

- So

+ so, what's a bloody bushdoctor?

- you don't wanna know

Bicameral Man

i wake up early in the morning

i get up early in the morning and i get down on my knees and pray
and after i've been finished with that i'll wash up
and i'll rummage in my kitchen

i take a tylenol p.m.
with mango juice and egg yoke in the morning
i call it
i call it an ave maria

and i go outside and i run
i run ... until ... my legs ... can run no more

i sit outside and i sweat in the hot sun
until the beads dribble down my face and i must squint

i squint my eyes and i marvel at the rainbow tinted brilliance
sparkling ovals of syncopated reflection
sunflare thru eyelids' half squint

in mid day
i write rhymes
i write poems
i ... write dreams in yoga journal

and i eat lunch

i
go to my local denny's
always denny's

definitely denny's

and i
have them cook me
steak and eggs

one t-bone steak medium raw

one raw egg cracked onto hot skillet

just bring me the skillet

and pickapeppa hot sauce

i would tell you what i do at night

but

you don't wanna know

Homecoming

this is the true story of S. Juarez,
a marine sergeant stationed in Iraq

headed home from the front and he forced to test luck
made the first phone call to his mother in months
swore to make the holiday a date to not miss
already been commissioned now he Sergeant Juarez

he had the camouflage with the bootstraps on
and 86 kills with one rifle alone
told him it was a smooth ride crossin the city in a convoy
two trucks and four humvees

a suicide bomb detonated from the rear
the blast is kickin the humvee in the air
a private in the backseat grabbin his ear
could see the driver face shredded when the smoke cleared

another soldier and he shoutin' cause he think he struck blind
tell him to stay calm, keep the strategy wise
and when the young serge checkin' on the convoy line
two rockets hit either side at the same time

head spinnin from a buck shot grazin his jaw
metal shard in his back the size of a baseball
and Juarez is charged with adrenaline rise
pullin the driver free why he feel so light

ripped open the door, it was
it was shreds in his pants where both his legs should be
gave him a handgun, fire if you can squeeze
told him one shot kills cause its gotta be

now his eyes getting heavy and the legs feel weak
left side running blood from a severed artery
thinking yo this is it, guess I lied to my moms
never shoulda promised I was gonna make it back home

feeling like giving up, heard a blast in the sky
a cobra jet fighter is raining the gun fire
hot shells was ringing, now he got the joy shout
saw the chopper spray the crowd then he passed out

scream awake like a needle that's scratchin a cross fader
a naval hospital but it was two weeks later
a fly young nurse with a Puerto Rican flavor
plenty of rest, chicken soup to get your weight up

blessed with the luck from a rosary charm
cold sweats in the night still hearin' the bombs
squad leader lost a leg but he glad he ain't gone
and this migraine is pounding like a gravity bong

homeboys from grade school, eyes that seen the beast
the pressure to take the medal to his moms and his niece
another folding flag, another dream
and asking her why your son died, why not me

some of these guys had kids and wives and families
their night mares got nightmares, can't hardly sleep
ringing the doorbell just the chaplain and me
now i'm screaming why your son died why not me

On Fasting

fasting is for self-control
for obedience
and for temperance

i fast to remind myself of the hunger

my spirit's craving to walk closer with God

fasting is there to restore balance

so, if i've eaten a big meal,
or had many large meals over a few days,
i'll fast for a day to return to my normal self

we must be careful to only satiate the senses
as much as we've chosen to

otherwise the physical becomes the master
and our mind and spirit become the slave

do not be enslaved by the senses

productive fasting strengthens the soul

so if i need to get ready for a powerful event,
or i'm just tired of feeling weak

fasting helps

i say productive fasting
because it is important to pray and meditate
as much as possible while on a fast

when i fast i eat nothing
(maybe a handful of rice
here and there,
depending on how many days
the fasting continues)

and i drink nothing but water

the water is important

but you can choose to refrain from anything
for a period of time, as long as that thing is
central to one of your desires
use the time to bring you closer to home

closer to balance

closer to your center

above all things
hold on to the center

Lifemind

A new song

Verse 1: I call it lifemind wired man
Seeking teachers, claimin' it when they pump hands
The evolution of mind fishing to understand veils of man
Flaming domes, passing homes that don't want it man
Controlling lands
Torch and make your heart blaze
The inner fire got me charged with the sharp phrase
They still denying my name
Livin' in shame till the cock crows
Owe me now thrice
Cause ya now puts it down with the yogi tao Christ
Wordplay pounds thru the whole of the night
Cause your boy goes hard like the old third reich
The sword of a knight be my third eyesight
Known to eat an m.c. like an old bowl of rice
The game seems to me all bark no bite
Had to resurrect the flame for my homeboy Christ
And never for the fame, joules spit drop the hit get the pentagon right
Keep my heart pure of gold and my pen game tight

I call it lifemind wired man

Whachu, whachu call it god?
Whachu call it god, whachu call it god, whachu call it god,
Wha-what? I call it life mind, wired man,
Whachu, whachu, whachu call it god…

Verse 2: It was electric charge and it was light
Feel the energy hard fizzin my spine all day all night
Bone marrow feelin charged with the thoughts of the most high
And I swear to you you see me you'll see it all in my eyes
Bear the overseein of a yogic state of mind
And I don't carry the cross
I carry the shine
Yogananda brought the flame to the lazur-west mind
The yoke is easy and the burden is light

The love of god the mind of Christ
The love of god the mind of Christ
The love of god the mind of Christ,
The burden is light, the burden is light.

The love of god the mind of Christ
The love of god the mind of Christ
The love of god the mind of Christ,
The burden is light, the burden is light.

{this is one of the mantras I came up with that proved really helpful for some of my pupils in the past. You just sit down Indian style and repeat this over and over in your head. Do it for long enough and you'll see some things.}

I call it lifemind, wired man

Whatchu, whatchu callitgod?

Verse 3: I, I wake up early in the morning reciting the "auto b of a yogi"
{that's yogananda's book}
Flip thru my Bible only Gideon version
I got "the prophet" {Kahlil Gibran, remind me to send you my copy of this}
on my mind never rush the funk
Black soap to the face with the "dharma bums" {Jack Kerouac}

I study teachings of "siddartha" with cinnamon toast cereal
Nothing that could be sweeter than the "bhagavad gita" {Hinduism}
Got the Koran in my bag just to keep me crunk
Had to thank "zarathustra" {Nietchsze}
cause he packed my lunch

Travel "the black whole" {that's one of my books}
for when "nausea" {jean paul sartre} rings
Answer the cycle phone with the art of zen things
{"Zen and the art of motorcycle maintenance", a definitely good read.}
Step into my zone with the "story of b" {Daniel Quinn}
Rip the underground show with my mic tai chi

My samuri eye's what the "hagakure" teach
Got the Lao Tzu crib with the Coltrane swing
and guarunteed to meditate daily, lotus pose, open palm technique
While flippin thru my notes, "Celestine prophecy" {Redford is the author}

I call it life mind wired man

Whatchu, whatchu call it god, ….